Hair of the Dog
— to —
Paint the Town Red

The Curious Origins of
Everyday Sayings and Fun Phrases

Andrew Thompson

Published in the US by
ULYSSES PRESS
PO Box 3440
Berkeley, CA 94703
www.ulyssespress.com

ISBN: 978-1-61243-668-5
Library of Congress Control Number: 2016957516

20 19 18 17 16 15 14 13 12 11 10 9 8 7

Printed in the United States

Acquisitions editor: Bridget Thoreson
Managing editor: Claire Chun
Editor: Shayna Keyles
Proofreader: Renee Rutledge
Layout: Caety Klingman
Front cover design: what!design @ whatweb.com
Cover artwork: © Angela Jazmine
Interior artwork: see page 256

To Felix

CONTENTS

INTRODUCTION
Start from Scratch: Meaning Versus Origin

As mad as a hatter…A son of a gun…To bite the bullet…To be saved by the bell…To be given short shrift…

Have you ever wondered where the phrase "in the limelight" comes from? Or what "cat got your tongue" originally meant? Who was it that painted the town red in the first place? It's time to find out.

Phrases from the English language cover every facet of life, but often their meanings don't correlate to their origins. In case you weren't aware, military tactics, nautical procedures, politics, entertainment, literature, and an array of other fields form the basis of many expressions that are used today. People are unwittingly quoting history on a daily basis.

The varied and bizarre explanations of our everyday phrases never cease to amaze and intrigue people—and probably confuse the life out of anyone whose second language is English.

Did you know that to "freeze the balls off a brass monkey" is in no way offensive, but actually relates to cold temperatures causing cannonballs to fall onto the deck of a ship? Or that to eat humble pie originally meant that you were eating offal and entrails, known as "umbles," instead of meat? Everyone knows what letting the cat out of the bag means, but did you know it originates from unscrupulous market vendors substituting cats for more valuable suckling pigs?

Most people simply don't have time to consider the origins of every phrase and idiom that we utter. We take our language for granted out of necessity, yet many of us are intrigued to know more. And that's where this book comes in.

There is often conflicting evidence and more than one possible origin of many phrases. In some cases, the discussion of a single expression could fill half the pages in this book. For these phrases, the most compelling view has been chosen. But that is not to say that there are no other possible explanations; these complicated situations just add weight to how intricate our language really is.

Hair of the Dog to Paint the Town Red explains the fascinating origins of 400 phrases that we use every day, breaking them up into different categories that will take you on a journey through every aspect of the world. What you'll read is both weird and wonderful, eccentric and funny—and at times downright unbelievable.

So stop barking up the wrong tree, don't rest on your laurels or turn a blind eye, and don't pass the buck. This book will ensure that you never look at the English language in the same way again—from when you start from scratch right up to the bitter end.

CHAPTER 1
As the Crow Flies:
The Nautical World

Batten Down the Hatches

MEANING: prepare for trouble or hard times

IN CONTEXT: Here comes the boss and he's in a bad mood. We'd better *batten down the hatches*.

Batten down the hatches is a nautical phrase that dates back to the early 1800s. Most sailing ships at the time had cargo holds that opened to the deck via hatches, sometimes called hatchways. These hatches were normally left open or simply covered with a grate that allowed for ventilation. When seas were rough or bad weather was imminent, the ship's captain would call to batten down the hatches to protect the cargo and prevent the hold from getting filled with rain or seawater. The hatches would be covered with canvas tarpaulins that would be held down with strips of wood, known as battens, to stop them from blowing off.

Cut and Run

MEANING: avoid a difficult situation by leaving abruptly

IN CONTEXT: The business was failing so instead of injecting more money, he decided to *cut and run*.

Cut and run originated in the early 1700s when the anchor cables of ships were made of rope. To raise an anchor took significant time and effort, especially in deep water. If a ship was at anchor and suddenly came under attack, the time taken to raise the anchor could be costly. To save time and escape with minimal damage, the crew would cut the anchor rope with an ax and allow the ship to run with the wind and escape to safety. The expression was being used figuratively by 1861 when Charles Dickens included it in his novel *Great Expectations*.

First Rate

MEANING: the very best quality

IN CONTEXT: When it comes to universities, Princeton is *first rate*.

First rate is a naval expression dating from the time of King Henry VIII. It was during his reign that the British Navy began organizing its ships according to their size and strength. The warships were rated on a scale of one to six. A small ship with little armory was considered sixth rate, while a large and well-armed ship was classed as first rate. The expression soon came to be used to refer to anything of the highest quality.

Square Meal

MEANING: a nutritious meal

IN CONTEXT: Jenny had been dieting for a month so was really looking forward to a good *square meal*.

Square meal is yet another nautical phrase. British warships in the 17th century had poor living conditions: The quarters were cramped, and most meals were insubstantial. In particular, breakfast and lunch usually consisted of little more than bread and water. However, the final meal of the day did provide some sustenance and generally included some form of meat. This meal was served on a large square tray made of wood, designed in that shape for easy storage. This larger, more nutritious serving became known as a square meal.

Whistle for It

MEANING: a request where you're unlikely to receive what you want

IN CONTEXT: After buying lottery tickets for years without any luck, I figured I was better off *whistling for it*.

Whistle for it has its origins in a sailing superstition. Some sailors believed that they could summon the wind on a calm day by whistling for it. The hope was that the wind would blow in sympathy with the sailors and fill the sails so the ship could move on. Others disagreed and believed that whistling was devil's music. They feared that whistling for the wind would result in a violent storm. Given that a gentle wind or a fierce storm rarely appeared, the expression came to mean what it does today.

Hunky Dory

MEANING: everything is fine and okay

IN CONTEXT: The IRS audited the company's books but found that everything was *hunky dory*.

Hunky dory began with a group of American sailors in the 19th century. There was a major street in Yokohama, Japan, called Honcho-dori. It was well-known for housing ladies of ill repute, and when in port after a long voyage, the sailors would frequent the street to partake in the recreational activities being offered. Hunky, meaning "sexy," was a play on the similar-looking word, Honcho, and when "dori" was added, a phrase was spawned.

Have Someone Over a Barrel

MEANING: helpless; at someone's mercy

IN CONTEXT: The police had captured the crime on camera, so they really had the accused *over a barrel*.

To **have someone over a barrel** alludes to the maritime practice of rescuing a drowning sailor. Once hauled from the water, the other crew members would place the sailor facedown over a barrel in order to empty his lungs of water. The sailor would be rolled back and forth in an attempt to expel  the water. Being completely helpless, and often unconscious, the sailor was totally reliant on the other crew members to save him.

Cut of Your Jib

MEANING: a person's general appearance and demeanor

IN CONTEXT: I'm not sure why I don't like Rod. I think it's just the *cut of his jib*.

Cut of your jib is another expression with naval origins. In common use by the early 1800s, it was used in an idiomatic way in 1824 by Sir Walter Scott in his novel *St. Ronan's Well*.

The jib of a sailing ship is the triangular sail set at the front of the boat. Each country had its own style of jib sail, so the nationality of a ship and whether it was hostile or not could be determined from its jib. Coupled with this, the jib was thought to be a good indication of the condition of the boat. The jib was responsible for the overall performance of the ship, so a well-cut jib suggested a high-quality ship.

Three Sheets to the Wind

MEANING: very drunk

IN CONTEXT: Doug had been at the bar all day, and when he came staggering home he was *three sheets to the wind*.

Three sheets to the wind has nautical origins. Originally "three sheets in the wind," this phrase relates to the sails of tall ships. The sails are controlled by ropes known as "sheets," which are fixed to the lower corners of the sails to hold them in place relative to the wind. If the sheets break or come loose, the sheets are said to be "to the wind." If three sheets are loose, the sails will flap wildly about. Having three sheets to the wind will result in the boat becoming completely out of control, much like a stumbling drunk.

Footloose and Fancy Free

MEANING: free from care or responsibility; unattached and single

IN CONTEXT: Hank and his girlfriend had parted ways, so he was *footloose and fancy free* at the party.

Footloose and fancy free is an expression whose origin lies with the early sailing boats. The "foot" is the bottom part of a sail that is connected to the boom. Sometimes in strong winds, it would become detached from the boom and was regarded as footloose. A footloose sail would flap around and be free to move whichever way the wind blew. It was considered footloose and fancy free.

As the Crow Flies

MEANING: in a straight line; the shortest distance between two points

IN CONTEXT: It's only five minutes *as the crow flies*, but it'll take you an hour to get up that windy road.

As the crow flies is a nautical phrase that dates to the time of the early English explorers. With few navigational aids and no maps, it was important to be able to find land while at sea. The crow was renowned as an intelligent bird that would always fly straight to the nearest food source, which meant land. Ships would always ensure they had a cage full of crows before they embarked on their journey. A crow would be released from the "crow's nest" at the top of the mast and the captain would follow the path it took, usually resulting in the fastest route to land.

Tide You Over

MEANING: to supply someone with something they need for a short period

IN CONTEXT: We were able to secure bridge financing to *tide us over* until our formal loan was approved.

Tide you over has its origins with the sea and, as the phrase suggests, the tide. In the absence of any wind to propel a ship via its sails, captains would use the tide to move the ship. The rising tide was also used to lift a ship over a threatening obstacle, such as a reef or sandbar. The first known usage of the phrase was by the British Captain John Smith in his 1627 book *A Sea Grammar*, where he wrote "To tide ouer to a place, is to goe ouer with the Tide of ebbe or flood, and stop the contrary by anchoring till the next Tide." The expression was being used figuratively by the early 1800s.

Between the Devil and the Deep Blue Sea

MEANING: between two undesirable alternatives

IN CONTEXT: I had a bad toothache, but the trip to the dentist was going to be painful too—I was caught *between the devil and the deep blue sea*.

Between the devil and the deep blue sea derives from traditional wooden sailing boats. Sailors used hot tar to seal, or caulk, the seams between planks to prevent leaking. The seam between the two topmost planks on the ship's side was known as the "devil" seam. It was the longest seam and closest to the water, so it needed regular sealing. This required a sailor to stand at the very edge of the deck or even be suspended over the side. If there was a sudden gust of wind or a large swell, the sailor could get knocked over the edge and find himself between the devil and the deep blue sea.

Hard and Fast

MEANING: rigidly adhered to; inflexible

IN CONTEXT: The rules for the fire drill were *hard and fast* and could not be altered.

Hard and fast is a nautical phrase. When a ship has run aground and is firmly beached on land, it is considered hard and fast and is unable to move until the tide comes in. The term was defined in William Henry Smyth's 1867 nautical dictionary *The Sailor's Word-book* as "said of a ship on shore." The term dates from the 1800s and was used in a figurative sense since that time as well.

Long Shot

MEANING: an attempt that has little chance of success

IN CONTEXT: He knew her agreeing to come to the dance was a *long shot*, but he decided to ask her anyway.

Long shot has its origins in naval warfare of the 1800s. Battleships carried cannons as their major weapons. Though very effective when they hit their targets, the cannons were inaccurate and the cannonballs could only travel relatively short distances. For this reason, most battles took place in fairly close quarters. Any shot that was fired at a ship outside the normal range was considered a "long" shot and unlikely to succeed.

Know the Ropes

MEANING: well versed in something

IN CONTEXT: He's been an engineer for twenty years and he really *knows the ropes*.

To **know the ropes** finds its origins with early sailing vessels. The sails on the ships of the 1600s were controlled by a myriad of ropes and knots, which were all connected in a complicated web. Sailors had to learn the intricate rigging required to raise, lower, and maneuver the sails in order to speed up, slow down, and change direction. The ropes were in constant use, and to fully master these tasks took years of experience. It was only then that a sailor could claim to know the ropes. The phrase was being used figuratively by the late 1800s.

Touch and Go

MEANING: a risky or precarious situation

IN CONTEXT: Walter almost didn't make it through the surgery. It was *touch and go* there for a minute.

The expression **touch and go** is another that derives from the sea. When traversing shallow water, a ship's keel might clip a reef or the seabed. If luck is on the captain's side, the ship may avoid disaster and move on unaffected instead of being completely grounded—it might touch and go. The saying was explained in William Henry Smyth's 1867 nautical dictionary *The Sailor's Word-book*, where he wrote, "Touch-and-go, said of anything within an ace of ruin; as in rounding a ship very narrowly to escape rocks, &c., or when, under sail, she rubs against the ground with her keel, without much diminution of her velocity."

By and Large

MEANING: in general; on the whole

IN CONTEXT: The final weekend has been wet, but *by and large* the month has been dry.

By and large is a nautical expression that harks back to the days of sailing ships. To sail "by" means to sail facing into the general direction of the wind, while sailing "large" is the most favorable condition and means to have the wind behind the ship. When the wind was constantly changing around, a captain would be required to sail by and large—both with the wind and against it. By doing this, the ship would continue to progress, but its path was not as direct or accurate.

Bitter End

MEANING: the absolute end; the last extremity

IN CONTEXT: Tim stayed at the party until the *bitter end*.

Bitter end is a nautical phrase and has nothing to do with either the taste or the ingredient used in some drinks. Centuries ago, the anchors of sailing ships were fixed to the decks by solid posts. These posts were known as "bitts." The sailors tied colored cloth to the end of the anchor rope near the bitt so that when the cloth was reached, the men knew they could not let the anchor out any farther. The small area of rope between the cloth and the bitt was called the "bitt end," which became known as the bitter end. When the rope was let out to the bitter end, it meant that no more rope remained to be used and the water was too deep.

Show Your True Colors

MEANING: reveal your true intentions or personality

IN CONTEXT: Most people can play the nice guy for a while, but eventually they will *show their true colors.*

Show your true colors is another nautical expression. In early 18th-century naval warfare, the flag of a ship's home country was called its colors. Under the *Articles of War*, published in 1757, ship captains were obliged to run up their country's flag when going into battle in order to identify the nationality of the ship. But as a method of deceiving the enemy, unscrupulous captains would run up a different flag, perhaps to fool the opposing captain into believing they were an ally. By doing this, the ship was able to get within firing range. With the element of surprise on his side, the captain would only then hoist his actual flag and show his true colors before firing on the enemy to gain an advantage.

Dead in the Water

MEANING: without any chance of success; stalled

IN CONTEXT: A hurricane was forecast for the coast, so our plans for a beach holiday were *dead in the water*.

Dead in the water is a nautical phrase dating to the days before engines were invented. Ships depended on the wind to propel them, and on days when there was no wind to make it come alive, the ship would remain stationary and be considered dead in the water. This had the potential to become a literal expression, particularly if the ship was under attack from the shoreline.

Loose Cannon

MEANING: a person who is unpredictable or out of control

IN CONTEXT: You'd better steer clear of Chip when he's been drinking. He's a real *loose cannon*.

Loose cannon is another sailing-related phrase. From as early as the 1600s, cannons were mounted on the decks of sailing ships and were used as the primary weapon in battles. As they were very heavy, it was essential for the cannons to be firmly secured. This was often done by mounting the cannons on rollers and fastening them down with ropes. In times of rough seas, or as a result of the violent recoil caused by firing the cannons, sometimes a cannon would break free of its restraints. The loose cannons would roll dangerously around the deck, causing damage to the ship and injury to the sailors.

In the Offing

MEANING: likely to happen soon; imminent

IN CONTEXT: Helen's interview went very well and she was sure a job offer was *in the offing*.

In the offing is a nautical expression originating in the early 1600s that came into widespread usage by the late 1700s. The offing is that part of the sea that is visible from, or off, the shore—the area between the shore and the horizon. In other words, a ship that was in the offing was within sight. A lookout who was watching for a ship to arrive would see it approaching when it was in the offing and would know that it would be docking fairly shortly.

Cat Got Your Tongue?

MEANING: silent or lost for words

IN CONTEXT: You're not saying much there, Bill. *Cat got your tongue* or something?

Often directed at someone who is silent but expected to speak, **cat got your tongue?** is the common truncation of "has a cat got your tongue?" While some claim that the saying began merely as an imaginative way of speaking to children, the likely origin stems from the sea. In the 17th century, the British Navy used a whip called cat o' nine tails for administering physical punishment aboard the ship. The whip was multi-tailed and inflicted incredible pain. When sailors were flogged, the pain was often so severe that it rendered the victim speechless.

On the Right Track

MEANING: to do something correctly or well

IN CONTEXT: Overtaxing the rich will not put the economy *on the right track*.

On the right track is an expression that has been corrupted from its original form. It has nautical origins, and was originally on the right "tack." In order to progress into a headwind, a sailing ship follows a zigzag style of path, angling left to right as it moves forward. This type of course plotting is known as "tacking." Tacking is a technical art, and a captain must be precise in order to avail himself of the wind. It is important to stay on the right tack because otherwise, the ship will make little or no progress.

Freeze the Balls off a Brass Monkey

MEANING: very cold weather conditions

IN CONTEXT: It's almost zero degrees out there, cold enough to *freeze the balls off a brass monkey*.

Cold enough to **freeze the balls off a brass monkey** has disputed origins, but the nautical explanation is the most compelling. Naval artillery guns in the 18th century required gunpowder and were manned by so-called powder monkeys who were usually young, agile boys, able to move easily though the tight passages. They would ferry the powder from the ship's hold to the guns. Next to the guns were brass triangles that supported stacks of cannonballs. By association with the young boys, these became known as brass monkeys. The advantage of brass was that it wasn't as corrosive as iron, but in cold weather it would contract more than other metals. On particularly cold days, the brass racks would contract, increasing their openings and causing the balls to fall through.

Hand over Fist

MEANING: quickly; at a fast rate

IN CONTEXT: The customers were lining up out the door and Bob was making money *hand over fist*.

Now used primarily in relation to making fast money, **hand over fist** is an expression with nautical origins. It was originally hand over hand when it began in the early 1700s, and was used to describe the fast progression of a sailor climbing up or hauling in a rope, one hand quickly going over the other. It was later modified to hand over fist, describing the flat hand passing over the fist that clenched the rope.

Turn a Blind Eye

MEANING: to knowingly ignore a situation, fact or reality

IN CONTEXT: He always took a long lunch break, but I *turned a blind eye* because he was such a good worker.

The British Naval Admiral Horatio Nelson is credited with the phrase **turn a blind eye**. Nelson had one blind eye. During the 1801 Battle of Copenhagen, Nelson and his superior, Sir Hyde Parker, disagreed over the tactics in fighting the large Danish-Norwegian fleet. At one point, Parker sent a signal by way of flags for Nelson to disengage from the battle. But Nelson was confident he could win. He deliberately held his telescope up to his bad eye and said, "I really do not see the signal." He continued the attack and secured a decisive victory.

Pass with Flying Colors

MEANING: success at a difficult task

IN CONTEXT: John passed his final exam *with flying colors*.

Pass with flying colors is a sailing term that dates back to the early 1700s. A ship's flag or banner was known as its colors. When a ship or a fleet was successful in battle and was returning to its homeland, it would sail in with its flag flying high on the mast. This indicated that the ship had been victorious: It had retained its flag rather than lost it to the enemy. To pass with flying colors was a sure sign of victory.

Give a Wide Berth

MEANING: keep at a safe distance; avoid

IN CONTEXT: Chad was the meanest guy in the school, so I always *gave him a wide berth*.

To **give a wide berth** dates to the 1600s and is another mariner's term. A berth is a place where a ship is moored at anchor, either in a harbor or out at sea. Once at berth, a ship will then float around with the tide or the wind, but only as far as the length of its anchor rope. When anchoring a ship in a harbor, the best way to prevent it from getting hit by other boats was to give them a wide berth so that they had enough room to move with the tide. Similarly, when maneuvering around another moored vessel, it was prudent to give it a wide berth so as to avoid any collision if it did move with the tide.

Spick and Span

MEANING: fresh and unused; neat and clean

IN CONTEXT: When Fran finished cleaning the house, it was all *spick and span*.

Spick and span is an expression that originated in the 16th century shipyards. The two words are now obsolete, but at that time a spick was a nail or spike, and a span was a wooden shaving or woodchip. When a ship was brand new and first launching, its nails would be shiny and rust free, and there would still be the odd wood shaving on the deck—it was considered all spick and span.

Flog a Dead Horse

MEANING: to engage in a fruitless effort

IN CONTEXT: Tony could not convince the crowd of his point of view, so he decided to stop *flogging a dead horse* and he sat down.

Flog a dead horse, or beat a dead horse, is a mariner's term and derives from the "horse latitudes," an area with irregular and unreliable winds about thirty degrees to either side of the equator. It is an area of high pressure that can result in weak winds and long periods of calm. Sailors were paid an advance wage at the start of a voyage and the time it took to pay the advance off was known as "dead horse" time. Because of the lack of wind, it sometimes took months to pass through the horse latitudes. This was advantageous to the sailors, as they had already received a payment, so they saw little point in working hard to get clear of the area—to do so would have been flogging a dead horse.

Under the Weather

MEANING: to feel unwell

IN CONTEXT: I couldn't make it into work yesterday as I was a little *under the weather*.

Under the weather is an expression with seafaring origins. Seasickness was a major problem in the early days of sailing before medication was invented to combat it. The ailment was particularly prevalent in times of rough seas and bad weather, when the ship would move about more violently. The greatest sway on a ship is on the deck and the most stable place is underneath near the keel. If a sailor became ill he was sent down below to recover—under the deck, and under the weather.

Turn the Corner

MEANING: pass a critical point after a difficult time; begin to recover

IN CONTEXT: Interest rates started to rise as the economy finally *turned the corner.*

Turn the corner relates to two treacherous oceanic corners—the Cape of Good Hope at the southern tip of Africa, and Cape Horn at the bottom of South America. At both of these capes, two oceans collide and the seas are violent and dangerous. It was always a worrying time when early sailing ships had to negotiate those rough waters, but once the ships had turned the corner, the sailors knew that they were in for some calm, plain sailing.

In the Doldrums

MEANING: to feel unmotivated or depressed

IN CONTEXT: I was feeling *in the doldrums* so I decided not to go to the party.

In the doldrums relates to a region by that name which is located slightly north of the equator between two belts of winds. The winds meet there and neutralize each other, which results in ships becoming stranded and sitting around idly, virtually unable to sail. Many assume that the expression comes from the name of this region, but the region was actually named because of its nature. "Doldrum" comes from the Old English word *dol*, meaning "dull." Though the Doldrums is now known as the Intertropical Convergence Zone, the phrase "in the doldrums" has been used in the figurative sense since the early 19th century.

Your Ship Has Come In

MEANING: when one becomes rich and successful

IN CONTEXT: When *my ship comes in* we'll buy a new house and car.

Dating from the mid-1800s, **your ship has come in** is a seafaring expression about investing in ships. A man might spend all his money in building a ship, fitting it out, and hiring a crew. The ship would then set

sail for a long voyage in the hope of recouping the money. It may be away for years at a time and the investor, unable to communicate with the captain, would never be sure if he was going to make any money or even see the ship again. It would only be when the ship reappeared that he would know the outcome. If laden with a cargo of valuables from faraway places, it would be said that his ship had come in.

Taken Aback

MEANING: startled or surprised by a sudden change

IN CONTEXT: I was completely *taken aback* when Claire left me. I just couldn't believe it.

Taken aback is a phrase related to sailing. Aback means facing toward the rear, and the sails of a ship are said to be aback when the wind flattens them against the supporting mast. A sudden wind change can slow a ship down, and in some cases drive it backwards. If such a change in wind causes a sailing ship to turn unexpectedly into the wind, the ship has been taken aback. This expression has been used in its literal sense since the late 17th century.

Leave High and Dry

MEANING: stranded without hope of recovery

IN CONTEXT: By the time I came back from the bathroom all my friends had left the party, *leaving me high and dry*.

To **leave something high and dry** is an expression that dates from the early 1800s. It originally related to a ship being run aground and unable to move. This left the ship exposed and vulnerable to attack, and the captain was rendered helpless until the tide came in. Its first written usage was in *The Times* newspaper in London in 1796, where it was reported that "The Russian frigate Archipelago, yesterday got aground below the Nore at high water, which; when the tide had ebbed, left her nearly high and dry."

Son of a Gun

MEANING: a rogue; usually said to someone in a friendly way

IN CONTEXT: All the girls want you to take them out, you old *son of a gun*.

Son of a gun has its origins with the sea. Centuries ago, the British Navy allowed women to join sailors on long voyages and live on the ships. Sometimes the women were the partners of the sailors and sometimes they were prostitutes. Pregnancies were common, and most babies were born in a designated area behind the ship's gun. Many pregnancies were unplanned, and in a lot of instances, the child's paternity was unknown. In such cases, the child was listed in the ship's log as the son of a gun.

Money for Old Rope

MEANING: a quick and easy way to earn money

IN CONTEXT: I got paid to eat at the restaurant and do a report on it for the owners. It was *money for old rope*.

The expression **money for old rope** has a nautical derivation. In the 17th and 18th centuries, when sailing ships returned to port, the sailors would assess all the rigging to ensure it was still seaworthy. Any rigging that had been damaged during the voyage would be removed. While unsuitable for sails, some of it would still be in good condition and able to be sold onshore. The more senior members of the crew were given authority by the captain to claim the discarded rope and they were able to profit from its sale, literally making money for old rope.

Nail Your Colors to the Mast

MEANING: to display one's beliefs defiantly

IN CONTEXT: The judge was in the minority, but he *nailed his colors to the mast* and refused to give an inch.

Nail your colors to the mast derives from naval warfare in the early 18th century. A ship's captain would enter battle with his flag, or "colors," flying proudly from the main mast. However, if he wished to surrender, he would lower his colors to announce his position to the enemy. Sailors were also able to lower the flag in times of trouble, so if a captain was determined not to surrender, he would literally nail the flag to the mast so that nobody could lower it and offer a sign of defeat.

Raining Cats and Dogs

MEANING: very hard rain

IN CONTEXT: It started *raining cats and dogs* so we had to quickly pack up the picnic and leave.

Raining cats and dogs has a number of potential origins, but the seafaring one is the most compelling. According to an ancient nautical myth, it was believed that cats had an influence over storms, while dogs were a symbol of the wind. This belief was held by the Vikings: Odin, the Norse storm god, was frequently shown surrounded by dogs and wolves. This led the early sailors to believe that in any storm, the rain was caused by cats and the winds were brought by dogs. Raining cats and dogs came to refer to any heavy rain.

On the Fiddle

MEANING: someone not operating within the rules and getting more than their fair share

IN CONTEXT: The school bursar got sacked because she was *on the fiddle* and stole some money from the official registers.

Like so many expressions, **on the fiddle** has nautical origins. The dining tables on ships had raised edges, known as "fiddles," which were used to prevent the plates from sliding off the table during rough weather at sea. The sailors ate from wooden plates that were built with their own fiddles to stop the food from sliding off them. If a sailor selfishly overfilled his plate so that the food piled up over the edge, it was said that he was on the fiddle.

Shake a Leg

MEANING: hurry up, especially in getting out of bed

IN CONTEXT: Adrian was running late for his meeting so I told him to *shake a leg*.

Shake a leg has its origins with the British Navy in the 19th century. It was at that time that civilian women were first allowed on board Royal Navy ships to boost morale. The sailors would be roused at first light with the cry of "Shake a leg!" This was used to distinguish between the men and the women; if a smooth and shapely female leg was presented as opposed to a hairy sailor's leg, the lady was permitted to stay in her bunk until all the men were dressed and gone. To this day, shake a leg is still often used in an attempt to hurry a person out of bed.

Slush Fund

MEANING: money that has been put aside to be used for discretionary purposes, particularly in a political context

IN CONTEXT: The candidate had run out of money so the party had to delve into the *slush fund*.

Slush fund has its origins with the sailing ships of the 17th century. In those days there was no refrigeration, and salted pork was the standard sailors' fare. To make it more palatable, the pork was boiled up in large pots. Excess fat that rose to the top of the pots would be skimmed off and put into empty barrels. This extra fat was known as slush and the sailors would sell it to soap and candlemakers, sharing the profits to buy luxury items. In 1866 the US Congress applied the term to a contingency fund it had set up, and the term then took on its current meaning.

You Scratch My Back and I'll Scratch Yours

MEANING: to do someone a favor if they do one for you

IN CONTEXT: After recommending three new clients to John, he handed me $100 and said with a smile, "*You scratch my back and I'll scratch yours.*"

The expression **you scratch my back and I'll scratch yours** has its origins with the British Navy. During the 17th century, the punishments meted out to sailors for being drunk, absent, or disobedient were severe. One of the main forms of punishment was a lashing with a cat o' nine tails, a whip with multiple strands that could inflict brutal gashes on the recipient's back. The common practice was to tie the offender to the ship's mast in full view and have him flogged by another crew member. The crew members came to an understanding that they would only deliver light lashes and merely "scratch" the other's back, knowing that they would receive similar leniency if their turn came to be flogged later in the voyage.

At a Loose End

MEANING: idle, with no plans and nothing to do

IN CONTEXT: I was *at a loose end* on Saturday night so I decided to go to bed early.

At a loose end derives from tall sailing ships. Where there are sails, there are ropes, and on large ships there are hundreds of ropes. The ropes are essential to ensure the sails are firmly in place, but these ropes can often become loose and unraveled. It is a full-time job to check the ship's rigging for untied ropes and loose ends. Whenever the ship's captain found men sitting around doing nothing, he would make them check the ropes—they would find themselves spending hours working at a loose end.

CHAPTER 2
Take a Rain Check: Sports and Games

Knuckle Down

MEANING: to diligently apply oneself

IN CONTEXT: Nick failed his first two subjects at university so he knew it was time to *knuckle down* and study hard.

Knuckle down has its origins in the game of marbles. A marble, also known as a "taw," is held with a crooked index finger and flicked by the thumb. It is an essential rule of the game that the knuckle of the index finger must be placed down on the ground before taking a shot. The knuckle must also be placed in the exact position that the player's previous marble ended. A player breaking these rules will be quickly told to concentrate and knuckle down.

You Can Run, but You Can't Hide

MEANING: you can try to escape but will eventually be caught

IN CONTEXT: Hector owed the government $10,000. He knew he'd have to pay it soon as *he could run but he couldn't hide*.

You can run, but you can't hide is an expression attributed to the great heavyweight boxer Joe Louis, known as the "Brown Bomber." In 1941, Louis fought Billy Conn, a much lighter and faster boxer. Behind on the scorecard, Louis eventually knocked Conn out in the 13th round. Still champion, in 1946 Louis fought a rematch with Conn. Remembering how close Louis had come to losing his belt in the first bout, boxing writers asked Louis how he would combat Conn's fast "hit and run" strategy. Joe Louis responded, "He can run, but he can't hide." The champion won the fight by knockout in the 8th round.

Knock the Spots Off

MEANING: to beat easily; to outdo completely

IN CONTEXT: Our team *knocked the spots off* the opposition and won by thirty points.

Knock the spots off is an expression that began in America in the mid-1800s. Carnivals were commonplace all over the country at the time and the most popular sideshow was the shooting gallery. All comers would test their marksmanship skills. The most used target was a playing card, the face of which had spots or marks on it to indicate the suit or value of the card. The object was to shoot through all the spots and remove as many as possible. Anyone who could knock all the spots off a card would win a prize.

Win Hands Down

MEANING: win easily with very little effort

IN CONTEXT: We were up by twenty points at halftime and we ended up *winning hands down*.

Win hands down originated with the sport of horse racing. A jockey needs to keep a tight rein on his horse to encourage it to run, but when a jockey is so far ahead of the competition that he can loosen the rein and still win without needing his whip, he can place both hands back on the reins and rest them down comfortably. He can then canter to the finish line and win hands down. The saying was used in the literal sense from the mid-19th century and it developed into the figurative sense in the early 20th century.

Above Board

MEANING: legal; honest and open

IN CONTEXT: The real estate agent had a bad reputation for shady dealings, but I found him to be completely *above board*.

Above board is a gaming expression. In card playing, a board is an antiquated word for a table, as in sideboard. If a player drops his hands below the table, he could be accused of trying to cheat by swapping his cards. To avoid any such suspicion, it is essential for players to keep their hands above the table at all times where the other players can see them. If all players are above board, nobody can suggest any wrongdoing.

High Jinks

MEANING: excited and silly behavior when people are enjoying themselves

IN CONTEXT: Bert had been drinking and was singing and dancing and getting up to all sorts of *high jinks*.

High jinks was originally the name of a drinking game that was popular in Scotland in the 1700s. In the game, dice were thrown and the players were scored. The loser could either forfeit or drink a potent cocktail of alcohol, which was likely to make him inebriated and foolish. Walter Scott referred to the game in his 1815 book *Guy Mannering*, and the phrase had acquired its present meaning by the mid-1800s.

Add Another String to Your Bow

MEANING: to add more than one skill or opportunity

IN CONTEXT: He *had more than one string to his bow*, so when his football career ended early, he was able to fall back on his legal practice.

Add another string to your bow owes its origins to medieval times and the sport of archery. Many men were armed with a bow and arrows, which was an essential weapon used in hunting and in defense. In addition, competitions often sprung up between men as to who was the best shot (which is how the sport of archery came into existence). So as to never be caught short, prudent archers were advised to add another string to their bow. This second string was attached at the top of the bow and wound around the handle. If their first string snapped or was damaged, the archer had a backup string to get him out of trouble. This is how the expression *second string* came into being, as well.

Wild Goose Chase

MEANING: a fruitless chase for something; a hopeless quest

IN CONTEXT: All the police knew was that the suspect had dark hair so they were definitely on a *wild goose chase*.

Wild goose chase has its origins in horse racing. The sport developed in England in the 16th century, and its earliest form was much different from what we see today. A race began with a lead horse being set off, the rider taking any direction he chose. The other riders were then sent off in pursuit, leaving at precise regular intervals. The pursuing competitors did not know exactly what route the lead rider had taken, so they all set off in different directions like wild geese trying to follow their leader. William Shakespeare popularized the expression in his 1597 play *Romeo and Juliet*.

Hell Bent for Leather

MEANING: to go all out, willing to do anything to achieve a goal

IN CONTEXT: Two ambulances passed me on the highway weaving in and out of traffic and going *hell bent for leather*.

Hell bent for leather relates to horse riding. The word "bent" means to be determined, as in "bent on doing something." To ride a horse aggressively for long distances can push it beyond its capabilities and cause it injury or death. With either result, the horse is rendered useless and is destined to be skinned for leather. Someone who pushed a horse to those extremes would be said to be hell bent on turning it into leather. Others say that the constant whipping or spurring of a horse would be hell for the horse's skin, which would later be made into leather, or that riding hard would be hell for the saddle leather.

Wear Your Heart on Your Sleeve

MEANING: show all your feelings and emotions

IN CONTEXT: The coach always *wore his heart on his sleeve* and was very animated during the final match.

Wear your heart on your sleeve derives from medieval jousting matches. When a king's court held a jousting match, it was customary for the competing knights to dedicate their performance to the woman they were courting. To show that he was representing his sweetheart, a knight would wear the colors of the lady he was supporting in cloths or ribbons tied to his arm—he would symbolically wear his heart on his sleeve. The phrase was popularized by Shakespeare in his 1604 play *Othello* when he wrote, "I will wear my heart upon my sleeve."

Upset the Apple Cart

MEANING: to create a difficulty or cause an upset

IN CONTEXT: I told John what Paul had said about him, which really *upset the apple cart*.

Upset the apple cart has unlikely origins that lie with the sport of wrestling. During the 18th century, the "apple cart" was a slang term in wrestling circles for a man's upper body. To upset the apple cart was to throw an opponent down, which put him in a difficult position and often prevented him from winning. The expression was first recorded by Jeremy Belknap in 1788 in his *The History of New Hampshire*.

Have the Bit between Your Teeth

MEANING: take control of a situation

IN CONTEXT: I had procrastinated over the assignment for days when I finally *got the bit between my teeth* and finished it in one night.

Have the bit between your teeth is another phrase that comes from horse racing. Bit is derived from the Old English word meaning "bite," and is the mouthpiece in a horse's bridle that is used to control the horse's movements. When a horse is being ridden normally, the reins press the bit against the soft part of the horse's mouth, causing it to turn its head. However, if the horse grabs it so that the bit is between its teeth, it takes control away from the rider and the reins have no effect. It is then free to run how it chooses. The expression was being used by the late 1600s.

Aid and Abet

MEANING: to help or incite someone, usually in the commission of a crime

IN CONTEXT: Holly was reprimanded for *aiding and abetting* the boys who were fighting.

Aid and abet has its origins from the now-outlawed spectacle of bear baiting. The word "abet" derives from the Norse word *beita*, meaning "to bite." Originally called "bear abetting" in 14th-century England, a hungry bear would be tethered to a pole in a pit and set upon by trained bulldogs. The dogs would bite the bear until it was killed, but in so doing would often suffer casualties or fatigue. If one of his dogs was tired, the owner would often urge it to continue. It was said that he was abetting the dog to keep biting. After adding the common word aid, the phrase "to aid and abet" was coined by the late 18th century.

Below the Belt

MEANING: an unfair or underhanded tactic

IN CONTEXT: Bill had been told the information in confidence, so to bring it up during the argument was a bit *below the belt*.

Below the belt originated with the sport of boxing. The London Prize Ring Rules were drafted in 1743 by a boxer named Jack Broughton. These included not hitting a man when he was down, nor hitting any part below the waist. These rules were then updated and replaced by  the Marquess of Queensberry in 1867 into a formal code to put an end to dangerous fighting techniques. One of the rules was that no boxer must ever aim a blow at an opponent "below the level of his trouser belt." Below the belt soon came to be used figuratively to mean any unfair tactic.

Great White Hope

MEANING: someone or something expected to achieve great success

IN CONTEXT: The new medical research center was the *great white hope* in cancer treatment.

Great white hope has its origins in the sporting arena, in particular boxing. It also has racial connotations. Jack Johnson became the first African American world heavyweight boxing champion when he beat the Canadian Tommy Burns in a bout that took place in Sydney, Australia, in 1908. Racial animosity among white boxing fans was so intense that they called out for another white boxer to take back the title. To answer the call, James Jeffries, a white American boxer, came out of retirement to fight Johnson. Jeffries was billed as the Great White Hope, but he, too, was beaten by Johnson in 1910, triggering violent racial riots across the country.

Up the Ante

MEANING: to raise the cost or risk of an activity

IN CONTEXT: By doubling the police force in the city, the government was really *upping the ante* for would-be criminals.

Up the ante sprung up from the card game of poker. *Ante* is a Latin word meaning before or in front. At the start of a hand before any cards are dealt, players must place a bet called the ante; that is, the up-front bet. As the hand progresses and cards are received, players can increase their bet, which is usually only done if a player has a good hand or is bluffing. Increasing the bet is known as raising the stakes or upping the ante. The expression has been used since the 1800s.

Take a Rain Check

MEANING: to decline an invitation, but leave the option to take it up another time

IN CONTEXT: I can't go with you to the cinema on Saturday, but can I *take a rain check* and go next week?

Take a rain check derives from baseball in America. In the late 1870s, the attendance at baseball games during the wet winter months was low. Baseball had always been the great American pastime, but the fans did not want to shell out the full price of a ticket if there was a risk that the game would be washed out or reduced because of rain. To combat this, the game's administrators began the practice of allowing fans to leave because of bad weather up to a certain point in a match, and then reuse their ticket on another day. This way the fans did not forfeit the fare and got to watch an entire game. It was known as taking a rain check, and the concept was formalized in 1890 in the constitution of the National League.

Upper Hand

MEANING: obtain a dominant position or control of a situation

IN CONTEXT: Oliver was trying to stay calm, but his anger got the *upper hand* and he finally exploded.

Upper hand is a saying that began with a simple 15th-century game. It involved a staff or stick, and two or more contestants. The first person held the staff at the bottom and the next person placed their hand directly above. This happened in turn until the top end of the shaft was reached. The last person to place their hand on the end of the shaft was said to have the upper hand and was the winner. This practice was adopted in the 19th century on American playgrounds to determine which side would bat first in impromptu baseball games.

Don't Look a Gift Horse in the Mouth

MEANING: don't be critical or ungrateful for a gift

IN CONTEXT: The TV was free so I didn't question where it came from, as I didn't want to *look a gift horse in the mouth*.

Don't look a gift horse in the mouth derives from racehorses and horses generally. Horses were always considered valuable, but there were very few ways of assessing a horse's age before purchase. It was a risk to buy a racehorse that was past its prime or a work horse that was old. The most reliable way of determining a horse's age is from its teeth—as a horse ages its teeth wear down, but they also protrude forward and its gums recede. If a horse was given to you it was rude to look that gift horse in the mouth, because this suggested you were assessing its value. This is also the derivation of the expression *straight from the horse's mouth* to describe firsthand information, as well as *long in the tooth*, another equine teeth-related phrase meaning that someone is old.

Get Someone's Goat

MEANING: to annoy or anger a person

IN CONTEXT: The tap kept dripping all night and by the end it really *got my goat*.

Get someone's goat is another expression with bizarre origins. It relates to horse racing in America in the early 20th century. It was common for hyperactive horses to be given goats as stablemates because, for some unknown reason, goats had a calming effect on horses. This was particularly important at racetracks, where horses were stabled in unfamiliar surroundings. Horses often became attached to their goats, and on race days, unscrupulous punters or opposing owners would sometimes steal the goats. This would make the horse agitated and likely to perform poorly in the race.

Down to the Wire

MEANING: until the last possible moment

IN CONTEXT: I made it to the airport gate just as it was shutting. It really came *down to the wire*.

The expression **down to the wire** has its origins with horse racing. Before camera technology existed to determine the winner of a close-run race, a string was stretched across the finish line to assist the judges to see who crossed the line first. The string was called a wire, and whoever broke it first was the winner. An evenly run race was said to go down to the wire. Also used in foot races, the phrase was being used literally through the late 1800s and figuratively by the early 1900s.

Keep It Up

MEANING: continue to do something; encouragement to have someone continue a task

IN CONTEXT: He got all As in his mid-term exams and the teacher told him to *keep it up* for the rest of the year.

Keep it up dates from the 1700s and the game of badminton. The idea of the game is to hit a small piece of rubber attached with feathers, known as a shuttlecock, over a high net using small tennis-style racquets. The shuttlecock must not hit the ground at any time and if it does, the point is lost. Spectators at badminton events would often shout out to keep it up during the rallies.

Start from Scratch

MEANING: start again from the beginning, regardless of any prior work done

IN CONTEXT: My computer crashed and I lost my assignment, so I had to *start from scratch*.

Start from scratch originated from the sport of horse racing in the Middle Ages. At that time, a line was marked, or scratched, in the ground by a sword. The jockeys began the race behind the mark, and if it was found that any of them weren't following the course that was set out, they would be required to go back and start again from scratch. This progressed into foot races with handicaps, where weaker competitors were given head starts of varying degrees, while a contestant who started from a scratch in the ground was given no advantage. The expression developed into today's figurative sense, which was then adopted in golf as "swing from scratch."

Full Tilt

MEANING: at top speed; with maximum energy

IN CONTEXT: I was late for the bus and had to run at *full tilt* to catch it.

Full tilt originated with the medieval sport of jousting. Tilt derives from the Old English word *tealt*, meaning unsteady or leaning. In England, tilting was the early name for jousting. It involved two knights on horseback charging at each other at high speed in an attempt to topple an opponent off his horse by aiming a lance at him. This is also where the phrase "tilting at windmills" comes from in Cervantes' 1605 book *Don Quixote*.

Turn the Tables

MEANING: to reverse a situation and gain the upper hand

IN CONTEXT: Our team was behind until near the end of the game, when we *turned the tables* and won.

Turn the tables has its origins in the game of backgammon. In the 17th century, the game was known in England as tables; the two halves of the playing board  are still called tables today. At the time, there was a rule that allowed the players to turn the tables. This involved reversing the board so that the players would continue from their opponent's previous position. The first figurative use of the expression was in Robert Sanderson's *XII Sermons* in 1634 when he said "Whosoever thou art that dost another wrong, do but turn the tables: imagine thy neighbor were now playing thy game, and thou his."

Dead End

MEANING: an impasse, allowing no progress

IN CONTEXT: My job is a *dead end* with no chance of promotion.

While **dead end** might logically relate to a passage that has no exit as being "dead," it actually began with lawn bowls, a sport that has been played in England for centuries. In bowling, an end is one stage of a game when all players have bowled toward the "jack," which is the small white target ball. If the jack is driven out of the rink (the playing area) by one of the player's balls, the end cannot be continued and must be replayed. It is considered a dead end.

Crew Cut

MEANING: a closely cropped male haircut

IN CONTEXT: He wanted to stay cooler for the summer so he got a *crew cut*.

Despite many associating **crew cut** with the military, where the style is common, it actually originated with the sport of rowing. In the 1940s, university rowers at Yale and Harvard began wearing their hair cropped very short on the back and sides with a slightly longer, brush-like top. The style was soon adopted by other sportsmen at the universities, but it was the rowing crews who set the trend.

Well Heeled

MEANING: wealthy

IN CONTEXT: The cost of housing in the best part of town was out of reach to all but the *well heeled*.

The origins of **well heeled** lie in the sport of cockfighting. When the sport began, birds that were equipped with long and strong spurs were known as well heeled, the "heel" relating to the position of the spur on the back of the cock's foot. The cocks use their spurs to kill their  opponents, so a well-heeled cock is a dangerous bird. The first known reference to the phrase was in 1866 in the Iowa newspaper the *Dubuque Daily Herald*, where "game cocks well heeled" were mentioned.

Pass the Buck

MEANING: shift blame or responsibility elsewhere

IN CONTEXT: It was his mistake and he should accept the blame. He's always *passing the buck*.

Pass the buck originates from the game of poker. Poker became popular in America during the 18th century and players were always suspicious of any form of bias or cheating. To combat this, the card dealer was frequently rotated during a game. The person who was next in line to deal was given a marker, which was often a knife. The handles of most knives were made of buck's horn, so the marker became known as a "buck." When the dealer's turn was complete he would pass the buck. Silver dollars were later used as markers, which is probably where the term buck originated to denote a dollar. The US president Harry S. Truman famously displayed a sign on his desk that read "the buck stops here" to indicate that he was willing to take responsibility for governing America.

Couldn't Swing a Cat

MEANING: in a small and confined space

IN CONTEXT: Our new apartment was clean and well-lit, but it was so small you *couldn't swing a cat*.

The origin of **couldn't swing a cat** is often confused. Many believe it dates from the 17th century and relates to there not being enough room below a ship's deck to swing a cat o' nine tails whip, but it actually began two hundred years earlier from a bizarre form of sport. At some country festivals, live cats would be swung around by the tail and hurled into the air as targets for archers to hit. This was a popular spectacle, so if a festival was crowded it would be said that there wasn't enough room to swing a cat.

Palm Off

MEANING: to dispose of deceptively; passing something unwanted to another person

IN CONTEXT: I didn't feel like mowing the lawn so I pretended I was ill and *palmed it off* to my brother.

Palm off is an expression that originated with the world of card playing and involves cheating. In many card games, there is a dealer who deals cards to all the players, including himself. An adept dealer will know various tricks and may get a quick look at the card he is about to deal to himself. If it is a bad card that he doesn't want, he may hide it in the palm of his hand, then deal himself the next card in the hope that it will be better. By sleight of hand, he will then palm off the unwanted card to another unwitting player.

Point Blank

MEANING: to tell directly; to refuse completely

IN CONTEXT: She locked herself in the bedroom and refused *point blank* to come out.

Point blank has sporting beginnings and originated in France. *Point blanc* is French for "white mark," the bull's-eye or center of an archery target. A shot from a distance has to be aimed above the target to allow it to drop with gravity, but a shot point blank is close enough so that the flight of the arrow hits the target directly without any arcing. The expression later widened to refer to anything done at very close range, especially gunfire.

Come Up to Scratch

MEANING: meet the standard

IN CONTEXT: I think we'll have to let John go before his probation period is over. He just hasn't *come up to scratch*.

Come up to scratch has its origins in the days of bare-knuckle boxing. Fights used to take place in a large circle drawn in the dirt, which is why it's called a "boxing ring" today. Across the middle of the ring another line was drawn, or scratched, and the boxers faced off while standing on either side of it. If a boxer was knocked down, he was given a thirty-second count to come up to the scratch and present himself as fit and willing to continue the bout. If the boxer was unable to come up to scratch, the fight was over and he was the loser.

Left in the Lurch

MEANING: to be left abandoned in an awkward or difficult situation

IN CONTEXT: My boss quit midway through the project and I was really *left in the lurch*.

The phrase **left in the lurch** has its origins with an old French board game called *lourche*. It was played with dice and was similar to backgammon. If a player was left in a position from which he couldn't win, he suffered a *lourche*, which was a disadvantage. This concept was then brought into the card game of cribbage. In that game, if a player reaches 51 holes on the board before the other reaches 31, the trailing player is said to be left in the lurch. The phrase was being used figuratively as early as 1596, when it was included in *Have With You to Saffron-Walden*, a pamphlet written by Thomas Nashe.

Across the Board

MEANING: all encompassing; applying to all the individuals in a group

IN CONTEXT: The new government promised tax cuts *across the board*.

Across the board was coined in America in the early 1900s and first used figuratively soon afterward. The expression comes from the sport of horse racing. At race meetings at the time, a large board was used to display the odds of the horses in a race. The odds were listed on each horse to win (make first), place (make second), or show (make third). An across the board bet was when a punter placed an equal amount of money on a particular horse to finish first, second, or third.

Clapped Out

MEANING: worn out or exhausted

IN CONTEXT: The old car looked completely *clapped out* and like it couldn't drive another mile.

Clapped out has its origins in the cruel sport of hare coursing, which began in the 17th century and continues to this day. The sport consists of releasing a hare then having it pursued by a pair of greyhounds, who race each other to catch it. At times during its flight, the hare will periodically stop to catch its breath. When it does this, it usually sits up on its haunches and looks around. Being virtually exhausted, the hare breathes so heavily that its chest heaves in and out and its front legs move backwards and forwards at the same time. This gives the appearance that the hare is clapping, and that's what it's called in the sport. Once a hare is clapped out, the race will probably soon be over.

No Dice

MEANING: futile; nothing happening; used as a refusal to a request

IN CONTEXT: When Dan asked me to lend him $100, I told him "*no dice*, I don't have any money."

No dice began in America in the early 20th century. Gambling was illegal in many states at the time, so if a game was interrupted by a police raid, men went to great  lengths to hide their dice when challenged. Courts would often throw out illegal gambling cases if no dice could be proffered as evidence—no dice meant no conviction. This led some gamblers to even swallow their dice to avoid arrest. The expression was being used colloquially by the 1920s.

Blue Ribbon Event

MEANING: the best; the most distinguished

IN CONTEXT: Sue won *the blue ribbon* in the baking contest. Hers was by far the best.

Blue ribbon event derives from a combination of horse racing and politics. The highest award for merit in Great Britain is a knighthood, and the most distinguished order of knighthood is the Most Noble Order of the Garter. Recipients of this award wear a garter made of dark blue velvet ribbon. In 1846, an avid horse racing follower named George Bentinck sold all his racehorses to pursue a career in politics. In 1848 he was defeated in Parliament and only a few days later, one of the horses he had sold won the Epsom Derby, the most prestigious race in the country. Disconsolate, Bentinck was heard to lament his misfortune and referred to the Derby as "the blue ribbon of the turf."

At the Drop of a Hat

MEANING: something that happens suddenly, with little warning

IN CONTEXT: You had to be careful what you said to Lisa, as she would cry *at the drop of a hat*.

At the drop of a hat sprung up from 19th-century sporting contests. Sporting referees at the time usually wore hats, which they would raise in the air as a signal that an event was about to begin. As soon as the hat was dropped, the contest would start. This was most commonly used in horse racing and boxing, where an event would begin at the drop of a hat. The technique was also used in the American West, where a man would sometimes drop his hat as a challenge to fight another. As soon as the hat hit the ground, a fight was liable to begin.

The Bigger They Are, the Harder They Fall

MEANING: the more powerful and successful people are, the more they suffer when they experience defeat

IN CONTEXT: We decided to sue the mining company despite how much money it had, because *the bigger they are, the harder they fall*.

The bigger they are, the harder they fall is a phrase that originates from the world of boxing. Bob Fitzsimmons was a British heavyweight boxer and he coined the phrase. In 1900 he fought Ed Dunkhorst in Brooklyn, New York. Known as "The Human Freight Car," Dunkhorst was a giant of a man and weighed in at nearly 400 pounds for the bout. Fitzsimmons was not all that big for a heavyweight and when he walked into the ring and saw his opponent, all he could say was, "the bigger they are, the harder they fall." Fitzsimmons won the fight by knockout.

Chip on Your Shoulder

MEANING: a sense of inferiority or a perceived grievance

IN CONTEXT: Tracey had been passed over for another promotion and had a real *chip on her shoulder* about it.

Chip on your shoulder began in the schoolyards of America in the 19th century. If two boys argued and one wanted to challenge the other to a fight, he would place an actual chip of wood (usually a piece of bark or a small stick) on his shoulder and dare the other to knock it off. If the challenge was taken up and the chip was knocked off, a proper fight would ensue. This practice of spoiling for a fight by having a chip on your shoulder soon developed into the well-known expression.

Bottle It

MEANING: to lose your nerve or courage

IN CONTEXT: Matt was desperate to ask her out on a date, but he *bottled it* at the last minute.

To **bottle it** originates from the days of bare-knuckle boxing in the 19th century. A fighter always had a man in his corner who supplied water and encouragement between rounds to keep the fighter's energy and spirits up during a bout. This man was known as the "bottleman," because he carried with him the boxer's water. Without the bottleman and the necessary water, the fighter was unable to continue. In cases where the fighter was losing, he would sometimes tell his bottleman to sneak away with the water bottle, which would give the fighter an excuse to quit. In these cases, it was said that the fighter had "bottled it."

Throw Your Hat into the Ring

MEANING: take up a challenge; signal an intention to join an enterprise

IN CONTEXT: The investment seemed a little risky, but a few of my friends had put money in so I decided to *throw my hat into the ring*.

Throw your hat into the ring has its origins with boxing. In the early 1800s, prizefighters would tour the country and box at traveling fairs. They offered to take on all comers and gave the local men a chance to win

money if they could last the distance or beat their opponents. Anyone who fancied his chances in a bout against these "professionals" would throw his hat into the ring. The hats were placed in a pile by the referee and then shown to the crowd in turn as an invitation for the owner to come up and fight.

Battle Royal

MEANING: an intense altercation; a free-for-all fight to the end

IN CONTEXT: The Thrilla in Manila between Ali and Frasier became a *battle royal*.

Battle royal is an expression which originates from the blood sport of cockfighting. A popular pastime among all classes in England since the 12th century, Henry VIII even had a cockpit built at Whitehall Palace. The royal cocks were usually the strongest and best fighting birds, and the most celebrated spectacle was a particular event in which sixteen of the best birds were pitted against each other. They fought until the final eight remaining cocks entered round two. Round three was four birds, and the two victors of that battle would enter the final round. This last round, known as a battle royal, was fought until there was one victor.

Bandied About

MEANING: to make frequent and casual use of a name, word, or idea

IN CONTEXT: The rumors about Cathy were *bandied about* at the office all morning.

When something is **bandied about** it is often repeated from person to person. The phrase originates from the 16th century French game called *bander*. Bander was a forerunner to tennis and involved hitting a ball to and fro between two opponents. The Irish then invented a new team sport similar to modern-day hockey, where a ball was hit between the players using a bowed stick. It too was called bander, named after the French game. In fact, because of the bowed stick that was used, the term bandy legged developed to refer to someone with bowed legs. Shakespeare then immortalized the term bandy to mean "to and fro" in his 1606 play *King Lear*.

Nick of Time

MEANING: without a second to spare

IN CONTEXT: The train was running early and we caught it just in the *nick of time*.

The phrase **nick of time** began in England during the Middle Ages. At that time, there would usually be a tally man to keep score during team games. He would carry a "tally stick," and each time a team scored he would carve a small nick (a notch or groove) into the stick. If the winning nick  was added just before the end of the match, it was known as the nick in time. The expression later became known as in the nick of time.

CHAPTER 3
Carry the Can: Work, Trades, and Money

Get Fired

MEANING: to lose your job

IN CONTEXT: He was caught stealing the company's stationery, so he immediately *got fired*.

To **get fired** originated from a time in England when miners carried their own tools from job to job. Like today, stealing was a serious offence, and any miner caught taking valuable materials, such as coal, tin, or other ore, was immediately dismissed. So as to prevent them repeating their crime in another employment, their tools would also be confiscated and burned at the plant in full view of all the workers— their tools would literally get fired. Some suggest that the actual offender was set on fire in these instances, but it was likely just his tools. To get fired was far harsher and more humiliating than to get the sack (page 79), and was always the result of malicious behavior.

At Sixes and Sevens

MEANING: a state of disorder or confusion

IN CONTEXT: We hadn't slept for over a day so we were *at sixes and sevens* by the time we went to bed.

At sixes and sevens has its origins in the London livery companies. All the way back in 1327, The Worshipful Company of Merchant Taylors and The Worshipful Company of Skinners each received their charter within a few days of each other. They were the sixth and seventh companies listed. A dispute immediately arose as to which company would be placed sixth when the various companies went on processions around the city. The debate raged, but it was finally agreed that the two companies would swap between sixth and seventh place each year, resulting in confusion for some observers.

Fly off the Handle

MEANING: to get very angry; lose one's temper

IN CONTEXT: He's got such a bad temper. He *flies off the handle* for no reason at all.

Fly off the handle is an expression that began with the early American frontier settlers. The iron head of an ax has a hollow area into which the wooden handle is inserted. The handle is tightly fitted, but in conditions when the atmosphere is very  dry, like in middle America, the wood can shrink and the ax head loosens. When being vigorously swung, the ax head can sometimes fly off from the handle in an uncontrolled manner. Such a piece of iron hurtling through the air could be very dangerous. The phrase was first seen in the written form in 1843 in Thomas C. Haliburton's *The Attaché; or, Sam Slick in England*.

Knock Off Work

MEANING: to finish work

IN CONTEXT: He'd put in a solid day's work so I told him he could *knock off* early.

Knock off work has its beginnings with the American slave trade in the early 19th century. River boats transported slaves to and from the plantations. These boats were rowed by the slaves themselves. To keep the men rowing in unison, a drummer would beat out the rhythm on a block of wood. When it was time to change shifts, he would knock off a distinctive hit to signify it was time to stop. This was later used in English factories, where knocking a mallet on a wooden workbench indicated the end of a shift.

Up to the Mark

MEANING: acceptable; up to the required standard

IN CONTEXT: The restaurant promised quality burgers, and I had to admit that they were *up to the mark*.

Often used in the negative, **up to the mark** originated in 1697 when the Britannia standard was introduced. It provided that all gold and silver that satisfied a certain level of purity be stamped with a hallmark by the assay office. This proved the authenticity of the material and became a sign to jewelers and buyers that it was genuine. In the beginning, all precious metals were inspected at Goldsmiths Hall in London before the inspection process spread to other locations. If a metal was not considered of the required standard, it was rejected as not being up to the hallmark. This expression was later shortened, and people spoke of the metals being up to the mark or not.

Against the Grain

MEANING: against the natural flow; opposed to one's inclination

IN CONTEXT: We followed our partner's advice to invest, although it went *against the grain*.

Against the grain has its origins in the field of woodwork and carpentry. When wood is planed, sawed, or sanded along the grain, it results in a smooth finish. However, when done against the grain, or obliquely to it, the wood will tend to splinter or be rough. Working against the grain is also far more difficult and strenuous. The first written use of this expression was by Shakespeare in *Coriolanus* in 1607.

Tarred with the Same Brush

MEANING: having the same faults or bad qualities

IN CONTEXT: They're politicians so they're both dishonest— they're all *tarred with the same brush*.

Often used in a derogatory sense, **tarred with the same brush** has its origins in early sheep farming. It was common for a number of sheep within any flock to develop sores from  time to time. These sores were usually treated with a coating of tar, which was applied with a brush. The same brush was used on every sheep with an infection, but it was important never to use it on a healthy sheep so as to prevent the contamination of a healthy animal with a sullied brush. This way, it was only the infected sheep that were tarred with the same brush. The term became a commonplace expression by the early 19th century.

Dressed to the Nines

MEANING: wearing very fashionable or expensive clothes

IN CONTEXT: It was an upscale restaurant so Joanne was *dressed to the nines.*

The origin of **dressed to the nines** is one of the most disputed in all of phraseology. While many argue against it, it is likely that the saying derives from clothing. Tailors require a great deal of fabric to make the best suits, because all the fabric must be cut in the same direction and the thread of the cloth must be parallel with the vertical line of the suit. This results in a lot of waste; nine yards' worth of cloth is usually needed. An  alternative explanation is that the phrase relates to the 99th Wiltshire Regiment from the mid-19th century in England. They were known as "The Nines," and were particularly noted for their exquisitely smart uniforms and presentation.

See How It Pans Out

MEANING: to see what happens

IN CONTEXT: He'd put in his best effort at the performance but he had to wait a week to *see how the results panned out.*

See how it pans out is another expression that began with the mining industry. During the California Gold Rush of the mid-1800s, the early prospectors used the simple technique of panning to look for gold in the rivers and streams. A deposit of sand and gravel from a creek bed was scooped into a small metal pan, and then it was gently agitated with water so that the lighter sand washed over the side while the heavier gold remained in the bottom of the pan. A prospector would wait and hope to see how each attempt panned out.

Get Off Scot-Free

MEANING: to get off unpunished or without obligation

IN CONTEXT: He was caught stealing, but he *got off scot-free* and the judge only gave him a warning.

Get off scot-free has nothing to do with the Scottish, but derives from the Old English word *scotfreo*, meaning "exempt from royal tax." First used in the 11th century in medieval England, a "scot" was a tax levied on homeowners according to the size and quality of their land. Poor people whose houses were in unfavorable positions didn't have to pay the tax—they got off scot-free. By the 16th century, innkeepers also used a slate called a scot to mark up the drinks someone had consumed. To leave without paying was known as getting off scot-free. The saying developed further to mean getting away with anything at all.

Fair to Middling

MEANING: mediocre; okay

IN CONTEXT: The concert performance was *fair to middling*, but it could have been a lot better if the lead singer was on form.

Fair to middling originated in the cotton industry in America in the 19th century. Cotton varied in quality and the better it was, the more it could be sold for. To facilitate this process, commercial cotton was graded in categories ranging from good to poor. Middling was an average grade, just below fair in quality. If the cotton was classed as fair to middling, it wasn't considered the best, but it was a little above average. The expression came to generally mean moderately good and was used from the late 1800s.

That's Just the Ticket

MEANING: exactly right, or exactly what is needed

IN CONTEXT: We need a big car for all our luggage and the SUV was *just the ticket*.

Some believe **that's just the ticket** is a corruption of the French word etiquette, meaning "proper behavior," but the more likely origin is from the early 20th century, when tickets were distributed to the poor to provide them with essential items such as food and clothing. The tickets were specific to the goods being sought and would be exchanged with shopkeepers, who were known to say "that's just the ticket" when the person produced the correct one. This practice continued during and after World War II, when ration booklets were used for the same purpose.

Talking Turkey

MEANING: to speak frankly and plainly

IN CONTEXT: With the formalities of the meeting out of the way, it was time to *talk turkey*.

Talking turkey began in colonial times when the European settlers encountered the Native American Indians. Wild turkeys lived among the Indians and were soon considered a high-demand delicacy, and were often put up for barter. There is one account about this from an 1837  article in the *Niles' Weekly Register*. It recorded that an Indian and a white man went shooting one day and all they got was one turkey and one crow. Desperate for the turkey, the white man bargained with the Indian by saying, "You may have your choice: you take the crow and I'll take the turkey; or, if you'd rather, I'll take the turkey and you take the crow." The Indian thought about this and then replied, "Ugh. You no talk turkey to me a bit." The bargaining for turkeys that took place on a daily basis then became known as talking turkey. This soon came to mean any serious discussion.

Foot the Bill

MEANING: to pay for something; to pay the check

IN CONTEXT: My boss took me out to lunch and the firm *footed the bill*.

Foot the bill began in the 1400s and derived from the simple method of adding up the various components of a check, or bill, and writing the total at the bottom, or foot. Originally meaning to total the account at the foot, by the 1800s it had changed to today's colloquial use, which is to pay the check rather than add it up.

On the Breadline

MEANING: to be very poor

IN CONTEXT: Kevin lost his job and after his savings ran out, he was *on the breadline*.

On the breadline originated in America in the 1860s. Charles and Maximilian Fleischmann were brothers who revolutionized the baking industry and created the first commercially produced yeast. Their bakery in New York was also famous for the freshness and quality of its bread. While other bakeries would use any leftover bread to sell to the next morning's customers, the Fleischmanns would give away any unsold bread to the poor of the city. At the end of each day, a line of starving people would form outside the bakery and wait for the free bread.

Lame Duck

MEANING: an ineffective person or business; a weakling

IN CONTEXT: The new company CEO had no idea what he was doing. He was a complete *lame duck*.

Lame duck dates from the mid-1700s and began in the financial world. It originated with the London Stock

Exchange and applied to those who were bankrupt and could not pay their debts. They were forced to waddle out of Exchange Alley in disgrace, like lame ducks. The first known mention of the term in writing was by Horace Walpole's 1761 letter to Sir Horace Mann where he wrote: "Do you know what a Bull and a Bear and a Lame Duck are?" The expression transferred to America in reference to ineffectual politicians by the mid-1800s.

Fly by the Seat of Your Pants

MEANING: do something without planning, deciding on the course of action as you go along

IN CONTEXT: Most stock investors don't plan too much, they just *fly by the seat of their pants* and hope for the best.

Related to the expression "on the fly," **fly by the seat of your pants** derives from the world of aviation in the 1930s. Early aircraft had few navigational aids or sophisticated instruments. Flying was predominantly based on the pilot's judgment and feel of the plane. The largest point of contact between the pilot and the plane is the seat, so most of the feedback comes through the seat to the pilot. It was through the seat that the pilot could feel the reactions of the plane and fly it accordingly. The term (which was originally fly by the seat of your trousers, showing it had British origins) came into prominence in relation to Douglas Corrigan's 1938 flight from America to Ireland. In that flight, some of the plane's systems failed and Corrigan was forced to fly by the seat of his pants.

Carry the Can

MEANING: to reluctantly take the blame for something that has gone wrong and was not necessarily your fault

IN CONTEXT: Rich felt he was always *carrying the can* for his boss's mistakes.

Carry the can began with beer and soldiers. For years on military bases, it was the job of a low-ranking soldier to fetch the beer. He would be required to carry a large bucket (or can, in British English) of beer from the mess hall to a group of drinking men. The man carrying the can was responsible for both bringing in the beer and returning the empty can for refilling. Despite the menial nature of the job there was a great reluctance to undertake it, because if the slightest drop was spilled, the man was open to much ridicule.

Mad as a Hatter

MEANING: crazy or completely mad

IN CONTEXT: Old Fred has finally gone senile and is as *mad as a hatter*.

Mad as a hatter stems from the 18th-century practice of using mercury nitrate in the making of felt hats. Mercury nitrate is a highly toxic chemical and exposure to it often affected the nervous systems of hat makers, causing them to tremble and jitter. This led many to believe that the hatters were crazy, so the expression mad as a hatter developed. In fact, mercury poisoning is still known today as "mad hatter disease." While not being the origin of the phrase, it was popularized by the eccentric Mad Hatter character in Lewis Carroll's 1865 work *Alice's Adventures in Wonderland*.

Stone Broke

MEANING: having no money at all

IN CONTEXT: He went to pay the check at the restaurant when he realized he was *stone broke*.

Stone broke stemmed from medieval England when an inability to pay your debts was considered a cardinal sin and was the reason for many suicides. If skilled tradesmen failed to repay their debts, their tools would be repossessed and their stone work benches broken into pieces. This practice rendered the tradesmen unable to work. Coupled with this, offenders were sometimes sentenced to hard labor in prison, where they were forced to break up stones and rocks. Being stone broke later became associated with anyone who had no money.

Dead as a Door Nail

MEANING: obviously dead; not at all active

IN CONTEXT: Nothing ever happens in our little town. It's as *dead as a door nail*.

Dead as a door nail dates from around 1350 and relates to the trade of carpentry. At the time, metal nails were hand-tooled and costly. Wooden pegs were often used as a cheaper alternative, but in the homes of the wealthy, large-headed nails were used in the doors to make them stronger and able to wear the repeated opening and closing. The practice was to hammer the nail through the wood and then bend the protruding end over to secure it flat against the wood. This process was called clinching, and afterward the nail was "dead" and could not be used again. Charles Dickens referred to the phrase in his 1843 book *A Christmas Carol*.

Bank on Someone

MEANING: to completely trust or rely on someone

IN CONTEXT: Jordan was a strong defender and we could always *bank on him* to make the tackle.

Bank on someone is an expression that began in medieval Venice before the days of modern banks. At the time, Venice was the hub of world trade and men set up benches in the main plazas to trade the various world currencies that appeared in the city from merchants and travelers. These men acted like banks, and the Italian word for bench also happens to be banco. Traders would exchange currencies with these men, borrow from them, and even leave money with them while they were away. The men had high scruples and were universally trusted. They were regarded as men who could be banked on.

Filthy Rich

MEANING: very wealthy

IN CONTEXT: The *filthy rich* may be able to afford that sort of vacation, but I can't.

Filthy rich derives from "filthy lucre," an expression used since the 16th century. The word "lucre" means money and comes from the Latin *lucrum*, meaning profit. Filthy lucre was first used by the English scholar, William Tyndale, in his translation of the New Testament (Titus 1:11), where it meant money gained dishonorably. By the 1920s in America, money was jokingly referred to using the slang term "the filthy," and from there the very wealthy were soon called the filthy rich. In modern times, the negative connotations have softened and the expression is used to refer to anyone who is rich, rather than just those who obtained their money by dubious means.

Run of the Mill

MEANING: average or ordinary

IN CONTEXT: There was nothing special about the jazz musicians—they were just *run of the mill.*

Run of the mill originated with the early milling towns of England. These great mill towns mass produced wool and cotton, which was exported all over the world. It was an extremely large industry, and a mill's reputation and profitability was primarily based on the quality of the material it produced. Quality control checks were essential before the material could be sold, but anything coming directly from the mill without having been inspected and graded was known as run of the mill and was considered inferior and prone to imperfections.

Let the Cat Out of the Bag

MEANING: give away a secret

IN CONTEXT: Phil finally *let the cat out of the bag* and told us his wife was pregnant.

Dating from as early as the 16th century, **letting the cat out of the bag** derives from a time when unscrupulous market vendors sold false goods. One of their common deceptions was to substitute a worthless cat for a valuable pig. After showing the unwitting buyer a sought-after suckling pig, negotiations on price would begin and the pig would be placed in a carry bag. At some point when the buyer was distracted, the pig would be replaced for a cat. It was only when the duped buyer got home that the fraud was revealed when he let the cat out of the bag.

Gone Haywire

MEANING: to behave wildly; a complete mess

IN CONTEXT: The office computers *went haywire* and we ended up paying everybody twice.

Gone haywire owes its origins to the early 1900s in America. At the time, a strong and light metal wire was used to bale up hay. The wire was tautly affixed and, once cut, would spring and quickly tangle. The wire was only intended to be used for baling, and once removed, it was rendered useless and was usually discarded. However, some farmers would use the rusted wire to make boundary fences or mend tools or machinery. It was not suitable for these measures and generally resulted in giving the farm an unkempt and disorderly appearance.

Break the Ice

MEANING: to make a start or pave the way

IN CONTEXT: It was a very formal and tense dinner party, but I decided to *break the ice* by making a joke.

Dating from the early 17th century, **break the ice** relates to ship navigation. Before the development of road networks, ships were used as the main source of trade and transportation. During winter, many rivers and channels would freeze over and the ships would get stuck, unable to pass. As a gesture of goodwill, the receiving port would often launch small ships to break the ice and clear a path for the larger vessels. Specialist ships known as icebreakers were later developed and used for the exploration of the polar regions. These ships had powerful engines and reinforced hulls.

Sold Down the River

MEANING: betrayed, cheated, or misled

IN CONTEXT: I kept the whole day free because Jim had promised me a ticket to the baseball game, but he *sold me down the river* and gave it to someone else.

Sold down the river derives from the time of slavery in America. In the early 19th century when the slave trade was in full swing, wealthy estate owners in the northern Mississippi region would handpick the best slaves to live and work on their properties. These slaves were in close contact with the landowner's family, living on the property and preparing meals. The lives of these slaves were somewhat comfortable (relatively speaking)—they were often treated well, and were sometimes seen as respected members of the family. But any slave who caused trouble or was considered unsuitable for the landowner's family was put on a boat and sold down the river to the slave labor plantations on the lower Mississippi. There the conditions were much harsher, and life was cheap.

On the Level

MEANING: honest; reliable; trustworthy

IN CONTEXT: You can believe him as he's *on the level*.

On the level began with the freemasons, skilled stone workers of the 14th century. In any construction, it was acknowledged that a perfectly flat base was essential if the building was going to be structurally sound and of high quality. They developed an instrument known as a level, which was used to ensure a flat and true base from which to work. The level symbolized integrity in the building process, and on the level was soon adapted into the wider sense that is used today.

Peter Out

MEANING: dwindle or diminish; come to an end

IN CONTEXT: He worked hard at first but his enthusiasm soon *petered out*.

Some suggest that **peter out** derives from biblical times and refers to the apostle Peter. When Jesus was arrested, Peter strenuously defended Christ, but by the next morning his enthusiastic support quickly diminished to the point that he even denied knowing Jesus. However, the likely origin of the phrase is from the early days of gold mining in America. Potassium nitrate, known as saltpeter, was a mineral ingredient in the explosives used in mining. When all the gold in a mine was exhausted, it was said to have petered out because the explosives had dwindled it down until nothing was left. The expression was being used literally and figuratively in America by the 1840s.

Barge In

MEANING: to abruptly intrude or interrupt

IN CONTEXT: His mother never knocks on his bedroom door. She just *barges in*.

Barge in began with the early days of transportation in England, before railways existed. The major towns of the country were connected by a network of waterways that allowed the movement of goods. The water was not very deep and the boats used on these waterways were flat-bottomed barges. This was the case since the 17th century and still continues today. The barges were cumbersome and awkward to steer, making collisions common as the vessels often barged in. The expression had gained its colloquial usage by the early 1900s.

No Such Thing as a Free Lunch

MEANING: you never get anything for nothing; there is always a hidden cost

IN CONTEXT: The store gave my son a free toy but I had to buy ten expensive batteries for it, which made me realize there is *no such thing as a free lunch*.

No such thing as a free lunch began during the 1840s in America. Bars and restaurants at the time began offering a free lunch to any customer who'd buy a drink. However, the free lunch was usually something insubstantial like a salty snack, which did little more than encourage the patron to drink even more and thus spend more money. It soon became apparent that after a free lunch, people were spending more money than if they'd just paid for a proper lunch in the first place. This technique became a lucrative way for establishments to make money, and many even advertised the free lunch in local newspapers.

Our Work Cut Out for Us

MEANING: a lot to be done; a difficult time lies ahead

IN CONTEXT: The government job required an enormous bid, so we knew we had *our work cut out for us* if we were to win it.

Our work cut out for us began in the 1800s when tailors began streamlining their operations. Traditionally a tailor would make a suit using one large piece of cloth, cutting the material and then stitching as he went. In order to make the work more efficient, the practice developed where a tailor's assistants would cut out the various patterns beforehand, leaving the tailor to stitch them together. At first this would seem to make the tailor's job easier, but it resulted in piles of cut material heaping up for the tailor to stitch. This made it difficult for the tailor to keep up, so if he had his work cut out for him, he had a very busy time ahead. The expression was first used metaphorically by Charles Dickens in his 1843 novel *A Christmas Carol*.

Hold a Candle

MEANING: to be far inferior to someone or something else

IN CONTEXT: Jeff is a fast runner, but he can't *hold a candle* to George.

Hold a candle dates back to the time before electricity. Usually expressed as "not fit to hold a candle" or "couldn't hold a candle," unskilled workers or apprentices were expected to hold a candle so that more experienced craftsmen had light while they undertook their work. Holding a candle was obviously not a very challenging role, so being told that you were not even fit to do that task placed you at the very bottom of the pecking order and as vastly inferior to the craftsman at work.

Make Ends Meet

MEANING: to live frugally, just within your means

IN CONTEXT: On such a low salary, Paul was only just able to *make ends meet*.

Make ends meet has its origins in the world of accountancy. From the 17th century, meet was an accounting term meaning match or balance. A bookkeeper's ledger contained two columns—one for expenditure and one for income. The ends were the bottom figures of those two columns. To make ends meet was to match the expenditure and income figures so that the books were balanced. By the mid-18th century, the phrase was in common usage in England in the figurative sense.

Hedge Your Bets

MEANING: to support more than one person or outcome to minimize the possibility of losing

IN CONTEXT: He *hedged his bets* and invested in both stocks and real estate.

Hedge your bets originated in 17th-century England. Landowners at the time would enclose pieces of their land by planting a row of trees and then pruning them to form a hedge. These hedges were normally made from the spiny Hawthorn bush, which formed an impenetrable barrier. This method acted as a means of protection against escaping animals. The hedges made the farmer's land more secure and limited his risk. The expression was first used in a financial sense as hedging one's debts in 1607 in John Donne's *Letters to Sir Henry Goodyer*.

Nineteen to the Dozen

MEANING: going at a very fast pace

IN CONTEXT: Lisa was very excited after getting her promotion at work, so she was talking *nineteen to the dozen.*

Nineteen to the dozen originated in the Cornish copper and tin mines in 18th-century England. Pumps were a necessary piece of equipment at the mines and were used to clear out the excess water that had been used in the mining or that had come in as a result of flooding. Hand pumps were used to clear the water until the advent of steam-driven pumps. While the traditional hand pumps were slow and labor intensive, the steam pumps were fueled by coal and were highly efficient. When running at maximum capacity, they could clear 19,000 gallons of water for every twelve bushels of coal burned.

Get the Sack

MEANING: to lose your job

IN CONTEXT: There was a downturn in business so we had to *give Stephen the sack.*

To **get the sack** derives from a time when tradesmen traveled from place to place looking for work. They generally owned their own tools and carried them around in a large sack. Work was often irregular, so the tradesmen never knew how long they might be employed. At the start of any given job they would hand over their sack to their employer to look after. The employer would keep the sack for the duration of the tradesman's employment. If the tradesman's services were no longer required and he was dismissed from the job, the employer would give him the sack.

Black Market

MEANING: the illegal buying or selling of goods to avoid governmental control; a place where illegal business is carried on

IN CONTEXT: I just bought all the latest music for next to nothing on the *black market*.

While there is some conjecture as to the origin of **black market**, the expression likely owes its beginnings to medieval England. At the time, nomadic mercenaries traveled the country selling their fighting skills to the highest bidder, usually noblemen who were raising armies. These men were weather-worn soldiers who lived solitary lives in the wilderness. Their armor was rarely polished, and being subjected to the elements, would oxidize into a blackish hue. As a result, they became known as the Black Knights. For sport, the Black Knights would sometimes compete in jousting matches against local men at country festivals, in which the winner would win his opponent's armor and weapons. Rather than carry around two sets of armor, the Black Knights would sell their spoils back to the loser, who would buy it at a cut-rate price. This after-market became known as the black market.

In a Shambles

MEANING: a state of complete disorder or ruin

IN CONTEXT: The mining boom was over and the economy was *in a shambles*.

In a shambles derives from the open-air meat sellers of medieval times. The word "shambles" derives from the Old

English word *sceamol*, meaning footstool, which came from the Latin *scamillum*, meaning small bench. Most towns at that time in England had streets designated to a single type of vendor. There were streets for grocers, bread sellers, and butchers, who all offered their wares from street-side workbenches. These streets were known as shambles, but it was the butchers that became particularly associated with the term. As they were supplied directly by the slaughterhouses, the meat shambles were renowned for being a complete mess of blood and offcuts. By the 1400s, the word "shambles" had become synonymous with general mess and disorder. The town of York in England to this day has a street called Shambles.

Burn the Candle at Both Ends

MEANING: to live or work at a hectic pace

IN CONTEXT: My final school assignment is due in a week so I've been *burning the candle at both ends* to get it finished.

To **burn the candle at both ends** began in France in the 1600s where it was written as brûler la chandelle par les deux bouts. The expression originally referred to domestic wastefulness. A candle was a valuable item, and to burn it at both ends would make it dwindle away quickly. The expression changed when it moved to England. In the days before electricity, tradesmen working late would secure their candles horizontally and light both ends. This would provide more light for them to work by, but it wouldn't last as long so they had to work faster. This also gave rise to the analogy of "burning up" your health by working too hard.

At Full Blast

MEANING: as loudly as possible; using full power

IN CONTEXT: The car stereo was *on full blast* so I couldn't hear a word the driver was saying.

At full blast dates to the days of the Industrial Revolution in the 18th century. Iron and other metals were essential commodities, and factories used huge blast furnaces to smelt the metals. Fuel was continuously supplied through the top of the furnace, while a hot blast of air was blown into the lower section, causing chemical reactions to produce molten metal. When the furnace was operating at full capacity and producing as much iron as possible, it was considered to be at full blast.

CHAPTER 4
Bite the Bullet: Military Matters

Back to the Drawing Board

MEANING: back to the beginning; to start again after the failure of an earlier attempt

IN CONTEXT: Billy assembled the toy car but its wheels wouldn't turn, so it was *back to the drawing board*.

Back to the drawing board began with a cartoon in the March 1, 1941 issue of the *New Yorker* magazine. A drawing board is an architect or drafter's table and is used to prepare designs. The cartoon, by the American artist Peter Arno, depicts a number of World War II military personnel running toward a plane  that has just crashed. There is a man in a suit holding a set of plans under his arm, walking away from the crash, and the caption reads, "Well, back to the old drawing board." By the late 1940s, the expression had become widespread and referred to any failed design.

Gung Ho

MEANING: eager and zealous

IN CONTEXT: Carl was excited and *gung ho* about his new role in the company.

Gung ho originated during World War II. It is an adaptation of the Chinese words *kung*, meaning "work," and *ho*, meaning "together." The term was anglicized by General Evans Carlson, who had spent time in China before the war. He adopted gung ho as a slogan for his US Marines unit known as the "Carlson's Raiders," who served in the Pacific region. The 1943 war film *Gung Ho!* told the story of the Carlson's Raiders and brought the expression into the mainstream. The film depicted the unit's sometimes reckless and irresponsible methods, which altered the meaning of the saying to what it is today.

Wreak Havoc

MEANING: to cause major destruction, disorder, or confusion

IN CONTEXT: The violent storms *wreaked havoc* up and down the coast.

To **wreak havoc** originated in 13th-century France. "Crier havot" was a military call that battlefield generals would make. *Havot* was the Old French word for "plunder." To *crier havot* meant the battle was won and the soldiers could begin the looting. The phrase reached England by the 14th century, where it had evolved to cry havoc. It was widely used, but in 1386, King Richard II banned the phrase on pain of death. The expression was later used by Shakespeare in a number of his plays, which propelled it into the mainstream before it was adapted to wreak havoc.

Face the Music

MEANING: to accept unpleasant consequences

IN CONTEXT: He had been on the run from the police for a month, but he decided to *face the music* and turn himself in.

Face the music has military origins. From the early days of the British army, errant soldiers were tried by court martial.

If a soldier was found guilty, he would generally receive a dishonorable discharge and be forced to leave the barracks. The disgraced soldier would be marched off the grounds in front of his comrades with a military drum squad playing. He was forced to literally face the music as he left. The expression "being drummed out" of the military also arose from this practice. Face the music has been used colloquially since the early 19th century.

Last-Ditch Attempt

MEANING: a final effort to solve a problem or avoid defeat

IN CONTEXT: The Tigers mounted one *last–ditch attempt* to win the game in the dying minutes.

Last-ditch attempt is a military term that dates to the late 17th century. King William III of England is credited with the expression during the Anglo-French War with the Dutch Republic. William was offered to be made Sovereign Prince of Holland if he would capitulate. He refused, and an envoy of the Dutch king threatened that William would witness the end of his state. "There is one way to avoid this," William replied. "To die defending it in the last ditch." The phrase was then picked up by the citizens of Westmoreland in the American War of Independence when in 1798 they proclaimed, "In war we know but one additional obligation:

to die in the last ditch or uphold our nation." By the early 1800s the expression was being adopted figuratively.

Hang Fire

MEANING: to wait before beginning something

IN CONTEXT: I was about to drive off but had to *hang fire* because the back door wasn't shut properly.

Hang fire originated in the 16th century when muzzle-loaded weaponry was used. When the trigger of a musket is pulled, a small quantity of gunpowder is ignited in an area called the priming pan. The flame from there burns through toward the barrel and sets off the main charge. Possibly because of the poor or inconsistent quality of the gunpowder, there was often a delay between the ignition in the priming pan and the detonation of the main charge that expelled the bullet. This period of delay was called the hang fire.

Hit the Ground Running

MEANING: get off to a quick and successful start; seize an opportunity

IN CONTEXT: The political party members promised to *hit the ground running* and not waste any time if they were elected.

Many believe that the expression **hit the ground running** originated from the two World Wars. Soldiers were trained to hit the ground running when leaving a moving boat, tank, or aircraft. This allowed the soldier to land on the ground smoothly, using the momentum of the craft so as to not lose his footing. However, it is more likely that the phrase existed before the 20th century and was used in America by stowaways jumping off a moving freight train before it entered the station, or from the Pony Express mail riders of the 1800s who were avoiding delays when they changed mounts.

Throw Down the Gauntlet

MEANING: to challenge someone

IN CONTEXT: I knew I could beat Matt in a race, so I *threw down the gauntlet* and he accepted.

To **throw down the gauntlet** derives from medieval times. A gauntlet was a glove that formed part of a knight's suit of armor. It was usually covered with steel plates, which aided in protection. If a dispute arose and a knight wanted to challenge someone to combat, he would throw down his metal gauntlet as a sign that he wanted a duel. If his opponent accepted the challenge, the opponent would pick up the gauntlet and the fight would begin. Taking up the gauntlet has since been used for accepting a challenge.

Rise and Shine

MEANING: get out of bed and prepare for the day

IN CONTEXT: We had a long trek the next day so the camp leader told us to *rise and shine* early and be ready by first light.

Rise and shine is a simple phrase that stems from the military. The "rise" is literal and means to wake up and get out of bed, usually before dawn. The "shine" derives from the shining of boots, buckles, and other equipment that soldiers were expected to do each morning before heading to the parade ground for inspection. It was, and still is, commonly preceded by a cry of "wakey, wakey" in many regiments.

The Whole Nine Yards

MEANING: the entire amount; as far or as much as possible

IN CONTEXT: My new TV was high definition and had 3-D technology—*the whole nine yards.*

The whole nine yards has disputed origins. As it's similar to dressed to the nines (page 62), some say it relates to the best suits being made from nine yards of fabric. But the more likely origin is military based. During World War II, the American fighter planes used 50-caliber machine guns that were fired from the doors by the gunners. The ammunition used by these guns was linked together on belts that were exactly nine yards long. If a target was shot at with the full belt of ammunition, it was said to have been given the whole nine yards.

Chance Your Arm

MEANING: to risk something

IN CONTEXT: I'd never invested in stocks before but I decided to *chance my arm* and have a go at it.

There is some conjecture over the origin of **chance your arm**. One school of thought is that it began with the military. Badges of rank were worn as stripes on the arm. Officers who took to the battlefield wearing their stripes were taking a risk, as these stripes could be easily noticed. Decisions the officers made could lead to either promotion or demotion—they were chancing their arm. An alternative explanation dates back to 1492 in Ireland. A vicious feud developed between two well-known families, the Ormonds and the Kildares. The Ormonds took refuge in St. Patrick's Cathedral in Dublin. The Kildares attacked, but then decided to make peace. The Ormonds were suspicious of the peace offering and refused to venture out. In an attempt to prove his good intentions, Gerald Fitzpatrick, the Earl of Kildare, cut a hole in the cathedral door and put his arm through, leaving it at the mercy of the Ormonds. But instead of cutting it off, James Butler, the Earl of Ormond, shook Fitzpatrick's hand and peace was made.

Beat a Hasty Retreat

MEANING: to withdraw rapidly; to leave quickly

IN CONTEXT: When the police arrived at the scene of the crime, the bandits *beat a hasty retreat.*

Beat a hasty retreat comes from the battlefields of the 16th century. While war at the time involved brutal hand-to-hand combat, it was generally governed by gentlemanly rules of fair play. A marching army would take its orders from the drummer, who would be stationed next to the commanding officer. There were a series of orders that the troops knew, and the drummer boy would beat them out so they all could hear and act accordingly. One of these drum beats was known as "The Retreat." At sunset, when the rules of engagement dictated that fighting would cease and the soldiers were to return to camp for the night, the drummer would beat The Retreat and the troops would return. In cases where the battle was not going well, the drummer would beat The Retreat faster to indicate urgency in the withdrawal.

Feather in Your Cap

MEANING: a symbol of honor or achievement; an accomplishment to be proud of

IN CONTEXT: Hal was very excited to be top of his class. It was a real *feather in his cap*.

Feather in your cap has its origins in the times of early warfare. In medieval England, knights who exhibited battlefield bravery were awarded feathers to be worn on their helmets. These were considered symbols of status, similar to the modern-day medals that soldiers receive. In the first major battle of the Hundred Years War in 1346, Prince Edward, the Prince of Wales, showed bravery. Known as the Black Prince, Edward was only sixteen years old when he was awarded the crest of John of Bohemia, his defeated enemy. The crest consisted of three ostrich feathers, which remains the crest of the Prince of Wales today. Other cultures (most notably many Native American tribes) have independently used the practice of placing a feather in the cap as a symbol of achievement. The phrase was used figuratively by the early 18th century and was popularized in "Yankee Doodle," the children's nursery rhyme, in the 1780s.

Bury the Hatchet

MEANING: to settle a conflict and make peace

IN CONTEXT: We'd argued for years, but we decided to put it behind us and *bury the hatchet*.

Bury the hatchet dates back to the times of the early European settlers in North America. Conflicts were rife as the white people encroached onto the lands of the Native Americans. When a truce was reached and an agreement made to stop the fighting, the Indians would literally bury all their weapons—axes, knives, tomahawks, and hatchets—in the ground so that they were no longer readily accessible. This was usually done by the chiefs of the tribe in a solemn ceremony that marked the end of the hostilities, and which the Native Americans considered binding.

On a Wing and a Prayer

MEANING: hopeful, but unlikely to succeed

IN CONTEXT: He is driving *on a wing and a prayer* in that old bomb of a car.

On a wing and a prayer is another expression that stems from World War II. The story goes that an American pilot flew back to base with one wing of his plane badly damaged. The other men at base were amazed that he hadn't crashed, and he told them he had been praying the whole way in. Another pilot then coined the phrase when he said, "a wing and a prayer brought you back." The saying got worldwide attention when it was referred to in two Hollywood films, *Flying Tigers* starring John Wayne in 1942, and *Wing and a Prayer* in 1944. "Coming in on a Wing and a Prayer" was also a patriotic song released in 1943 that popularized the expression. It described a damaged plane barely able to make it back to base.

Down a Peg or Two

MEANING: to humble someone who is conceited

IN CONTEXT: Don had always been at the top of the class but when the new boy beat him easily in the final exam, it took him *down a peg or two*.

To take someone **down a peg or two** has disputed origins. Some say it relates to the sea and how a ship's flag was raised and lowered by pegs—the higher the peg, the greater the honor. A more cogent origin dates back to the 10th century. King Edred of England  was in constant battle against the Vikings, but was concerned with the amount of alcohol his army was drinking. As a measure to keep his soldiers sober for battle, Edred directed that pegs be placed in the sides of beer barrels. No soldier was permitted to drink to below the peg in a single session. To get around this rule, soldiers started drinking from other men's barrels and this would take them down a peg or two.

Basket Case

MEANING: a person or thing that is in a completely hopeless or useless condition

IN CONTEXT: Within weeks of his divorce, Danny had become a complete *basket case*.

Basket case began as American military slang from World War I. It referred to soldiers who had lost both arms and legs and had to be carried in a basket. The Surgeon General of the US Army cemented the term when he issued a bulletin in 1919 stating that he "denies that there is any foundation for the stories that have been circulated of the existence of 'basket cases' in our hospitals." The term was later used to refer to people who suffered mental incapacities.

Flash in the Pan

MEANING: an ultimate disappointment after a promising start

IN CONTEXT: Tom won his first two tennis tournaments, but he turned out to be a *flash in the pan* as he never got past the first round again.

Flash in the pan has military origins from the 18th century. Flintlock muskets contained small priming pans that held charges of gunpowder. When the gun's trigger was pulled, a spark ignited the priming powder, which usually set off the main powder charge in the musket's bore and fired the weapon. In some cases, the priming powder failed to light the main charge. The priming powder would flash in the pan but no shot would be discharged, resulting in disappointment after a positive start.

Diehard Supporter

MEANING: one who stubbornly resists change despite a hopeless cause

IN CONTEXT: The Eagles hadn't won a game all season and it was raining heavily, but Ian was a *diehard supporter* so he went to watch regardless.

The phrase **diehard supporter** has military origins and comes from the Battle of Albuera during the Peninsular War in 1811. During the battle, the commanding officer of the 57th West Middlesex Regiment of Foot, William Inglis, was badly wounded and lay injured on the battlefield. The English were vastly outnumbered by the French and were under attack. Despite this, Inglis refused all attempts to carry him to safety and instead encouraged his men by shouting "Die hard, 57th, die hard." The English won the battle, and from then on the regiment was known as the "Die Hards." The phrase "diehard supporter" crossed into politics in the early 1900s to describe anyone who stood staunchly by a cause or colleague.

Pyrrhic Victory

MEANING: a victory gained at too great a cost

IN CONTEXT: It was a very divisive campaign and even though they won the election, it turned out to be a *Pyrrhic victory*.

Pyrrhic victory is a phrase that alludes to the Greek King Pyrrhus of Epirus. His army fought the Romans during the Pyrrhic War for the control of Magna Graecia. In the Battle of Asculum in southern Italy fought in 279 BC, Pyrrhus defeated the Romans but suffered severe losses, including most of his principal commanders. King Pyrrhus was later quoted as saying "Another such victory and we are lost." The expression was used figuratively from the late 1800s.

Over the Top

MEANING: to an excessive degree; beyond acceptable limits; outrageous

IN CONTEXT: There was a band and a free bar for 200 people—completely *over the top* for a 35th birthday party.

Sometimes now shortened to "OTT," **over the top** has its origins in trench warfare. In World War I, to go over the top was to charge on foot across open ground from the safety of the trenches. The order given was "over the top, lads, and the best of luck," but few had much luck as they ran head on into enemy machine gun fire. On the first day of the Battle of the Somme in July 1916, over 58,000 casualties were sustained by the British with this outrageous over the top tactic.

On Your High Horse

MEANING: to behave in a self-righteous manner

IN CONTEXT: He was in the wrong, so I told him to get down *off his high horse* and apologize.

On your high horse began with the army officers of medieval England. To assume a commanding position of supremacy, they would ride on large horses and look down upon those of a lower rank. The higher the officer's rank, the larger his horse. A large horse was also needed for such high-ranking men, as they generally wore heavy suits of armor and a strong horse was needed to bear the weight. Political leaders then adopted this idea as a symbol of power. They would parade through towns on large horses, which gave them an air of superiority as they looked down upon the common folk. The expression was first recorded by the English theologian

John Wycliffe in 1380, and by the 18th century it had changed and was being used metaphorically with mocking connotations.

Hold the Fort

MEANING: maintain things in the absence of others

IN CONTEXT: My parents asked me to stay home and *hold the fort* while they went out to dinner.

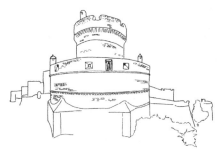

Hold the fort owes its origins to the American Civil War. During the Battle of Allatoona in 1864, General William Sherman was gathering his army atop Mount Kennesaw, near Atlanta, to fight a Confederate troop. He told General Corse that reinforcements were being mounted and to "hold the fort at all costs, for I am coming." While Sherman immortalized the phrase, it earned widespread acclaim in the late 1800s when the American composer and popular evangelist Philip Bliss wrote the gospel song "Hold the Fort."

Parting Shot

MEANING: a hostile gesture or remark made while departing, which the recipient has no chance to respond to

IN CONTEXT: She couldn't resist a *parting shot* on her last day of work, so she told her boss he was the worst lawyer she'd ever seen.

The origins of **parting shot** date back to a military tactic from the 17th century. The Parthians were an ancient race living in northeast Persia, and their army included mounted archers. The archers would ride away from the enemy at full gallop, giving the impression of a retreat. As the enemy approached, the archers, using superb equestrian skills, would turn and fire arrows backwards with great accuracy. Originally known as a "Parthian shot," the phrase was corrupted to parting shot by the early 20th century.

Ride Roughshod

MEANING: to treat harshly or domineeringly

IN CONTEXT: He *rode roughshod* over his friends to advance his own interests.

To **ride roughshod** has military beginnings. Horses that are roughshod have nailheads and sometimes metal points protruding from the bottom of their shoes. These are deliberately inserted to provide extra traction in wet or icy conditions. During the 18th century, it became common practice for cavalry soldiers to intentionally roughshod their horses. This turned the horses into brutal weapons, severely damaging the foot soldiers and horses of the enemy when they charged and rode roughshod over them.

Bite the Bullet

MEANING: bear up in a difficult situation, or carry out an undesirable task and move on

IN CONTEXT: Bruce hated his job so he finally *bit the bullet* and quit.

Many believe that **bite the bullet** originated during the American Civil War when soldiers, in the absence of anesthesia during surgery, would bite down on the malleable lead of a bullet to keep themselves from screaming. However, the real origin is thought to be from the Indian Rebellion of 1857. At the time, gun cartridges came in two parts. The projectile was inserted into a base and held in place with grease made from pig fat. To load the bullets, the two parts had to be broken apart and the base then had to be filled with gunpowder. Hindi soldiers were forced to bite the bullet and separate the two parts. They had to do this despite being required to bite into the grease made from pigs, an animal which they considered sacred.

More Bang for Your Buck

MEANING: better value for your money

IN CONTEXT: This cheaper car is just as fast as the larger model and gives you *more bang for your buck.*

More bang for your buck originated with the US national security policy in the 1950s under the administration of President Dwight D. Eisenhower. Known as the "New Look," the policy increased the military's stocks of comparatively inexpensive nuclear weapons in order to reduce the number of army personnel and the associated costs. In 1954, US Secretary of Defense Charles Erwin Wilson coined the phrase "more bang for your buck" when he used it to refer to the policy of using nuclear weapons, instead of a large army, to suppress the threat the Soviet Union posed to democracy. It is thought that the expression was an adaptation of Pepsi's advertising slogan, "more bounce to the ounce," which was introduced in 1950.

Molotov Cocktail

MEANING: a hand-held fire bomb

IN CONTEXT: The rioters were throwing *Molotov cocktails* at the advancing police.

The term **Molotov cocktail** began during World War II. The phrase was invented by the Finnish, who were referring to the Soviet foreign minister Vyacheslav Molotov. He was responsible for the partitioning of Finland under a pact with Nazi Germany, and many believed he was also responsible for the subsequent invasion of Finland in November 1939. There was much propaganda associated with the invasion, including the ludicrous claim by Molotov that the bombing missions were actually humanitarian food deliveries for the starving Finns. In response to this, the Finns referred to the Soviet cluster bombs as "Molotov bread baskets" and when they developed hand-held petrol bombs to throw at the Soviet tanks, they called them Molotov cocktails as a "drink to go with the food."

CHAPTER 5
On the Bandwagon: The Political Realm

Spin Doctor

MEANING: someone who gives a twisted and favorable version of events; a political press agent or publicist

IN CONTEXT: A good *spin doctor* could have made the scandal a lot less damaging.

Spin doctor has its origins in fairly recent American politics. The word "spin" has been in use since the early 1800s in relation to telling a story. James Hardy Vaux's 1819 book *A New and Comprehensive Vocabulary of the Flash Language*  referred to "spinning a yarn, signifying to relate their various adventures, exploits, and escapes to each other." But it wasn't until the 1980s that the full expression began. Ronald Reagan described the public relations officers to his Strategic Defense Initiative as being on "spin control" in providing a favorable version of events to the media. The phrase soon changed to spin doctor in the colloquial sense of someone who could repair something.

Blood, Sweat, and Tears

MEANING: hard work and effort in difficult conditions

IN CONTEXT: It took a lot of *blood, sweat, and tears* to plough the muddy field by hand.

Blood, sweat, and tears is said to have originated from John Donne's 1611 poem "An Anatomy of the World." It was later written by the Welsh minister Christmas Evans in his 1837 *Sermons on Various Subjects* when he referred to Christ being "bathed in his own blood, sweat, and tears." But it was Winston Churchill, the British Prime Minister and great orator, who brought the phrase to the people in a speech to the House of Commons in 1940. When speaking of the hardships that were sure to come during World War II, he said, "I have nothing to offer but blood, toil, tears, and sweat."

When It Comes to the Crunch

MEANING: the decisive point

IN CONTEXT: *When it comes to the crunch*, Sally will always tell the truth.

When it comes to the crunch began with British politics in the mid-1900s and is another expression credited to Winston Churchill. In the time leading up to and during World War II, Churchill began using the word "crunch" to describe decisive or challenging situations. A 1939 edition of *The Daily Telegraph* quoted him as saying, "Whether Spain will be allowed to find its way back to sanity and health depends upon the general adjustment or outcome of the European crunch." Churchill's usage of crunch in this sense soon spawned the full expression that exists today.

Bite the Hand that Feeds You

MEANING: to show ingratitude

IN CONTEXT: I was given a scholarship to the college so I decided not to *bite the hand that fed me* and refrained from criticizing its policies, even though I disagreed with them.

Generally used in the negative with "don't," the expression
bite the hand that feeds you is thought to date back to the
Greek poet Sappho in 600 BC, when she used the metaphor
of a dog biting its master. But the phrase is attributed to
Edmund Burke, the Irish statesman and political theorist.
Referring to public anger at the government for a food
shortage, he wrote in his 1795 memorandum *Thoughts and
Details on Scarcity*, "Having looked to government for bread,
on the first scarcity they will turn and bite the hand that
feeds them."

Bob's Your Uncle

MEANING: everything will be all right and a favorable result
will be achieved with very little effort

IN CONTEXT: Just fill out the application form, put it in the
post, and *Bob's your uncle*, you'll get your money.

Generally said to conclude a set of simple instructions,
Bob's your uncle dates back to 1886. In that year, Arthur
Balfour was unexpectedly appointed to the prestigious job
of Chief Secretary for Ireland. Many believed he was not
qualified for the job and didn't deserve it. As it turned out,
the then British Prime Minister, Robert Gascoyne-Cecile,
was Balfour's uncle. It was the Prime Minister's nepotism
that got Balfour the post, and as a result he went on to enjoy
a successful career in politics, even becoming Prime Minister
himself, all because Bob was his uncle. As a side note, the
word "nepotism" actually derives from "nephew," completing
the link.

Whistle Stop Tour

MEANING: a trip that makes stops in many places over a short space of time

IN CONTEXT: We traveled around the entire country in ten weeks—a real *whistle stop tour*.

Whistle stop tour stems from politics. During the mid-1900s in America, trains stopped at all the major towns, but they only stopped at small towns if a passenger requested it. Upon such a request, the conductor would blow the train's whistle twice to indicate a stop was approaching. During President Harry Truman's 1948 campaign, he traveled by train, stopping briefly at many places to deliver speeches. During his speech in Los Angeles, Truman joked and said that it was the biggest whistle stop town he had visited. The crowd loved it and the phrase stuck.

In the Bag

MEANING: a successful outcome is absolutely certain

IN CONTEXT: With only ten minutes to go, the lead was twenty-five points so the game was *in the bag*.

While there are conflicting theories on the origins of **in the bag**, including those relating to baseball and hunting, the early days of the British parliament is its likely birthplace. On the back of the Speaker's chair hung a velvet bag. All successful petitions that were brought before the House of Commons would be placed in that bag. Because it was known that all such petitions had been successful, they became known as in the bag.

Hear, Hear

MEANING: a strong signal of agreement or endorsement

IN CONTEXT: After a rousing speech in the British parliament, the members loudly shouted "*hear, hear.*"

Hear, hear originated in the British parliament in the late 17th century. In both the House of Commons and the House of Lords, if anyone disagreed with a speaker they would hum loudly to try to drown out the speech. But if any members were in agreement with what was being said, they would shout "hear him, hear him" in an attempt to make those humming men actually listen. It was later contracted to "hear, hear," and is still used in parliament today to signify the listener's agreement with the point being made. It is also thought to be said because applause is generally forbidden in parliament.

Nothing Is Certain Except for Death and Taxes

MEANING: only these two things in life are certain

IN CONTEXT: Don't write off victory just yet. *Nothing is certain except for death and taxes.*

Nothing is certain except for death and taxes had been written in various forms during the 1700s. In his 1726 book *The Political History of the Devil*, Daniel Defoe wrote: "Things as certain as death and taxes, can be more firmly believed."

However, it was Benjamin Franklin, one of the Founding Fathers of America, who coined the phrase and made it widespread. In discussing the new constitution in a letter to Jean-Baptiste Leroy in 1789, Franklin wrote: "Our new Constitution is now established, and has an appearance that promises permanency; but in this world nothing can be said to be certain, except death and taxes."

Toe the Line

MEANING: abide by the rules; submit to authority

IN CONTEXT: Steve had disobeyed his parents all month, so he decided it was time to *toe the line* and do as he was told.

Toe the line has political origins. In the British House of Commons, arguments often became heated. To deter members of opposing parties from attacking each other, two parallel red lines were marked on the floor. The lines were two sword lengths apart, and the members were required to stand behind their respective lines at all times. If any member did cross the line and approach the other party, he was ordered to retreat and toe the line. The lines still exist in the parliament today and the tradition remains, although nobody carries swords.

Off the Cuff

MEANING: to speak or carry out a task spontaneously, without preparation

IN CONTEXT: His speech was thirty minutes long and was entirely *off the cuff*.

Off the cuff is a phrase that relates to public speaking. In the 1800s, men wore shirts with detachable collars and cuffs, which made them easier to clean. Politicians and keynote speakers generally wanted to give an audience the impression that they were good speakers who could hold the people's attention without any preparation or the need to refer to notes. It was a common practice at the time to write notes on their shirt cuffs before a speech. Only they could see the notes, so the audience would be none the wiser. Politicians would also make additional last-minute notes on their cuffs to counter the arguments of their opponents.

Pie in the Sky

MEANING: a fantasy; an unachievable dream

IN CONTEXT: He always talks about setting up his own business but the plans are just *pie in the sky*.

Pie in the sky has American origins and was coined by Joe Hill in 1911. Hill was an instrumental member of the radical labor organization The Industrial Workers of the World, known as the Wobblies. He wrote a number of songs for the Wobblies, including "The Preacher and the Slave," which parodied the Salvation Army hymn "In the Sweet By-and-By." Hill's song criticized the Salvation Army's philosophy, in particular their desire to save souls rather than feed the hungry. The lines of Hill's parody were, "You will eat by and by, in that glorious land in the sky. Work and pray, live on hay. You'll get pie in the sky when you die."

On the Bandwagon

MEANING: to join in an already-successful venture

IN CONTEXT: Once it became apparent that Craig would win the election, everyone decided to jump *on the bandwagon* and support him.

To jump or climb **on the bandwagon** has its origins in politics. In 19th-century America, traveling bands and circuses would parade through towns on brightly colored, well-decorated bandwagons. They would often perform at political rallies and attracted large crowds of people. Because the bandwagons were usually the center of attention at any given event, wily politicians saw an opening. The politicians would often climb up on the bandwagon, interrupt the performance, and campaign to the captive audience below.

CHAPTER 6
In the Limelight:
That's Entertainment

Back to Square One

MEANING: to start again; back to the beginning

IN CONTEXT: Our planning decision was overturned, so it's *back to square one* for the entire project.

Back to square one began in the 1930s when the BBC in Britain began broadcasting soccer matches on the radio. *The Radio Times*, which was the BBC's listings magazine, published a numbered grid system which symbolically divided the playing field into eight rectangles. This allowed commentators to describe to listeners exactly where the ball was at any given time, allowing the listeners to follow the game without seeing it. Square one was at the goalkeeper, so whenever the ball was passed back to him and the play was about to resume, it was referred to as being back to square one.

Keeping Up with the Joneses

MEANING: striving to match one's neighbors in terms of possessions and wealth

IN CONTEXT: Evan didn't really need a new car but he bought one to *keep up with the Joneses.*

Keeping up with the Joneses originated from a popular comic strip of that name that was published in the *New York Globe. Keeping Up with the Joneses* began in 1913 and ran for twenty-eight years, bolstered by a 1915 cartoon film adaptation that played in cinemas throughout America. It was written by Arthur "Pop" Momand, and chronicled his experiences of living in suburbia. Jones was a common surname at the time and was meant as a generic term for "the neighbors." Years later, Momand wrote: "We had been living way beyond our means in our endeavor to keep up with the well-to-do class. I also noticed that most of our friends were doing the same. I decided it would make good comic-strip material. At first I thought of calling it Keeping Up with the Smiths, but in the end decided 'Jones' was more euphonious."

Ham It Up

MEANING: to show expressions or emotions more obviously than is realistic

IN CONTEXT: Johnny was really *hamming it up* when he told the story to his grandmother.

While there are a number of competing theories, it is widely accepted that **ham it up** derives from the world of theater in the 1800s. At that time, black and white minstrel shows were performed around America. These entertainers would sing a popular song called "The Hamfat Man," about low-paid and inept actors who had to use ham fat to remove their makeup after a show. From this, any bad acting became known as hamming it up. A similar theory is that the expression came from the 19th century actor Hamish McCulloch, who was known as "Ham." He led a touring troupe of actors around America who were said to give very poor performances.

Soap Opera

MEANING: a television serial drama; a real-life situation resembling one that might occur in a soap opera

IN CONTEXT: She's always talking about the boyfriends who've broken up with her. It's like one long *soap opera*.

Soap opera began in 1920s America. *Amos 'n' Andy* was a popular weekly radio show at the time, and one of the earliest comedy series. The show was for family listening, and was broadcast during prime time. Proctor and Gamble, a prominent soap manufacturer, saw the opportunity to obtain widespread exposure and began advertising their products during the breaks in the show. They then went on to sponsor the program. A trend soon developed, and other soap manufacturers began sponsoring similar shows. As a result, these serial shows were being called soap operas by the late 1930s.

Blonde Bombshell

MEANING: a glamorous woman with blonde hair, often a film actress

IN CONTEXT: That new girl in the mail room is a real *blonde bombshell* and has everyone talking about her.

The expression **blonde bombshell** originated in Hollywood in the 1930s. Jean Harlow was a highly popular, platinum-blonde American film actress and sex symbol at the time. In 1933 she was the lead in the Hollywood film *Bombshell*. The key advertising line for the film was "Lovely, luscious, exotic Jean Harlow as the Blonde Bombshell of filmdom." The term was later used to refer to other actresses, including Marlene Dietrich, Brigitte Bardot, Jayne Mansfield, and most notably, Marilyn Monroe. By the 1950s, the term had largely replaced "femme fatale" as a means of referring to the lead female role in a film.

Fit as a Fiddle

MEANING: fit and in very good health

IN CONTEXT: Frank's been training all summer and he's as *fit as a fiddle*.

Fit as a fiddle is a shortened version of the original saying "fit as a fiddler." A fiddle is the colloquial name for a violin. In medieval times in England, fiddlers would play energetic street performances to throngs of people. They would dance and weave through the crowd as they played. The best performers were physically fit and agile, hence the expression. Just why and when the saying was contracted is not known.

In the Limelight

MEANING: at the center of attention

IN CONTEXT: Ellen loves attention. She's always putting herself *in the limelight*.

In the limelight has its origins in the theater. When calcium oxide, more commonly known as lime, is heated, it produces an intense white light. This process was first used to effect by Thomas Drummond in the 1820s. He was a Scottish army engineer who used heated lime as an aid in map making because the bright light was visible at a distance. The technique was then adopted in theaters to illuminate the stage, and was first used in Covent Garden in London in 1837. The actors who were the center of attention on the stage were said to be standing in the limelight. This saying now applies to anyone who is the focus of attention.

Steal Your Thunder

MEANING: when someone takes credit for something you did

IN CONTEXT: I'd made the meal from scratch but Jan really *stole my thunder* when she served it to the guests.

Steal your thunder has its beginnings in the theater. In 1704 a literary critic and playwright named John Dennis had his play *Appius and Virginia* produced at the Theatre Royal, Drury Lane in London. For the show, he invented a novel method for creating the sound effect for thunder—he hit large tin sheets together back stage. While the audience loved the realistic sound effect, the play flopped and was replaced by *Macbeth*. When that production used his technique for simulating thunder, Dennis was enraged and was reported to have said, "How these rascals use me. They will not have my play and yet they steal my thunder."

Break a Leg

MEANING: used to wish someone, such as an actor, success in a performance, especially on opening night

IN CONTEXT: It was Rob's first night in the lead role, so everybody told him to *break a leg*.

Break a leg is said by some to be related to the assassination of Abraham Lincoln by John Wilkes Booth in 1865. This occurred at Ford's Theater in Washington DC, and Booth, a renowned actor himself, broke his leg while jumping onto the stage to escape. It is generally accepted that this is not the origin and that the phrase came into existence well before then. When a successful theater performance is applauded by an audience, the cast of a play will return to the front of the stage. This can happen a number of times, the curtain rising and falling on each occasion. The actors are required to bow or curtsy each time, bending or "breaking" a leg as they do. And the more times this happens, the more likely it is that they will trip and actually break a leg.

Cut to the Chase

MEANING: get to the point

IN CONTEXT: Julie's story was dragging on so I told her to *cut to the chase*.

Cut to the chase originated in the world of cinematography, specifically the silent films of the 1920s. In the early American film industry, many silent films had long-winded romantic story lines and ended in an exciting car chase sequence. A viewer who was bored and wanted to see the action might say "cut to the chase," in a plea for the projectionist to jump forward to the dramatic scene. This has continued through to modern times, where movie executives sometimes ask for a film to be advanced to the key scene so that they can make a quick assessment of its prospects.

Pull Out All the Stops

MEANING: to make every possible effort

IN CONTEXT: Zoe had bought a new dress, shoes, and bag for the party. She really *pulled out all the stops*.

Pull out all the stops stems from the musical world. Church organs used knobs to control the air flow through the pipes. These knobs were known as stops. When the stops were in, the air flow was less and the music not very loud. If there were many people in the congregation and the music was needed to be heard at the back of the church, the organist would pull out all the stops, which would increase the volume.

It's a Funny Old World

MEANING: indicating an acceptance of or resignation to a situation

IN CONTEXT: The postman arrived just after Ned had been to the post office to collect his mail. "*It's a funny old world*," he said to himself.

It's a funny old world was first used in the 1934 comedy film *You're Telling Me!* It starred W. C. Fields and at one point he says "It's a funny old world—a man is lucky if he gets out alive." The popularity of Fields quickly made the expression commonplace. It has been quoted ever since, notably by the British Prime Minister Margaret Thatcher after her decision to quit politics in November 1990. Alluding to the fact that she had never lost an election in her life yet had been forced to stand down, she said "It's a funny old world, isn't it?"

Put a Sock in It

MEANING: to tell someone to be quiet

IN CONTEXT: Max just kept yelling so I told him to *put a sock in it*.

Put a sock in it has its origins in the early days of radio broadcasts and sound recording. The equipment in the early 1900s was not very sophisticated, and the ability to control the volumes of the various instruments was limited. When orchestras were recorded in the studios, the horn sections were overpowering and completely drowned out the wind and string sections. To combat this and reduce their playing volume, horn players would stuff an actual sock into the mouth of their instrument. If he thought this damper necessary, a conductor would tell them to put a sock in it. By the 1920s the expression was being used colloquially.

Pleased as Punch

MEANING: delighted; very happy, sometimes in a smug way

IN CONTEXT: Joan got every answer in the quiz correct and was as *pleased as punch* about it.

Sometimes said using "proud," **pleased as punch** began with the Punch and Judy puppet shows. The main character, Mr. Punch, is depicted as a wife-beating serial killer, who derives great sadistic pleasure from his evil deeds, exclaiming "That's the way to do it!" whenever he dispatches another victim. The show began in Italy as *Pulcinella*, but soon became quintessentially English. Used in literature from as early as the 17th century, Charles Dickens refers to the expression in two of his books from the 1850s, *David Copperfield* and *Hard Times*.

Egg on Your Face

MEANING: a mistake, leaving one feeling foolish; to be embarrassed

IN CONTEXT: If you're going to confront someone, you'd better get your facts straight or you could end up with *egg on your face.*

Some suggest that the expression **egg on your face** originated in America in the 1960s when the opponents of a political candidate would throw eggs at him to make him look foolish. But the real origin of the phrase began long before that, in the Victorian era  of theater in the 1800s. In slapstick comedies at the time, actors made the "fall guy" of any production look foolish by breaking eggs on his forehead in an attempt to add humor to the spectacle.

Old Chestnut

MEANING: an old joke, story, or excuse that has been heard many times before

IN CONTEXT: Brendan said the dog ate his homework. What an *old chestnut.*

That **old chestnut** comes from the world of theater; in particular, it comes from William Diamond's 1816 play *The*

Broken Sword, which was staged in London's Covent Garden. In the play, Captain Xavier keeps repeating the same joke about a cork tree, albeit with minor changes, to Pablo, one of the other characters. Tired of this, Pablo interrupts and says, "It's a chestnut. I have heard you tell the joke twenty-seven times and I'm sure it was a chestnut." The expression became well-known years later when the American actor William Warren played the part of Pablo. He was at a dinner party when one of the guests began to tell an old joke. Warren interrupted the joke and, with much amusement, said, "It's an old chestnut, that's what it is."

In the Groove

MEANING: to function perfectly with little effort

IN CONTEXT: Glenn's performance was one of the best I've seen. He was really *in the groove*.

In the groove stems from the early vinyl records. Records are made with a number of grooves cut into the material where the music is recorded. The record is played by a stylus, or needle, which must sit neatly in the groove to ensure good sound quality. If a stylus is worn, making its tip too wide, it will not sit in the groove and the sound will become distorted. Equally, if the record is scratched, the stylus may slip out of the groove and the record won't play. The phrase took on its idiomatic qualities with the arrival of jazz in the 1920s. The free-spirited nature of jazz bands and the way the band members skillfully played in with each other led people to describe them as in the groove.

Life of Reilly

MEANING: an easy and pleasant life, without having to work hard

IN CONTEXT: Josh had saved up a lot of money, so he took the rest of the year off and lived the *life of Reilly*.

Living the **life of Reilly** (sometimes spelled "Riley") is an expression with musical origins. Pat Rooney was an Irish-American singer who had a popular song in the 1880s called "Is That Mr. Reilly?" It told the story of a character who claimed to be on the verge of being rich and was always describing the easy life he would lead if he came into money. However, it is generally thought that the phrase was brought to the wider public in a 1919 song written by Howard Pease called "My Name Is Kelly." In reference to the earlier song, the lyrics of My Name Is Kelly included, "Faith and my name is Kelly, Michael Kelly, but I'm living the life of Reilly just the same."

Sixty-Four Dollar Question

MEANING: a crucial question or issue

IN CONTEXT: Who will be the next president? That's the *sixty-four dollar question*.

The **sixty-four dollar question** began in American with the 1940s radio quiz show *Take It Or Leave It*. It ran from 1940 to 1947 and involved contestants answering increasingly difficult questions. After answering a question correctly, the contestant had the choice to either take the money being offered, or leave it and have a go at the next higher valued question. The first question was worth one dollar, and the value progressively doubled up to the seventh and final question, which was worth sixty-four dollars. The expression entered popular use in 1955 when the radio show moved to a more lucrative television program and became *The 64 Thousand Dollar Question*.

Put the Dampers On

MEANING: to make something less enjoyable; reduce the enthusiasm for something

IN CONTEXT: The torrential rain really *put a damper on* the outdoor Christmas party.

Put the dampers on has its origins in music. A damper is a device used on piano strings. It is operated by a foot peddle and presses against the strings. This reduces the sound of the piano. When the conductor instructed the orchestra to put the dampers on, he wanted to tone down the volume of the performance. This phrase is often mistakenly said using "dampener," probably because of the notion of water dampening out a fire.

CHAPTER 7
Purple Patch: Ancient Times

Two-Faced

MEANING: someone who is hypocritical, or shares one view with one person then a conflicting view with another

IN CONTEXT: Sue is so *two-faced*. She's nice to me one minute, then criticizes me behind my back the next.

Two-faced has its origins in Roman mythology. Janus was the Roman god of beginnings and transitions, and consequently gates, doors, and passages. He  was responsible for the gates of Heaven and was depicted as having two faces, one at the front of his head and one at the back. This gave him the ability to look to the future and into the past and to see both directions at once. The legend of Janus led Romans to believe that anyone who held opposing views simultaneously was also two-faced.

Wrong Side of the Bed

MEANING: said if someone is in a bad mood

IN CONTEXT: Roger was so grumpy this morning. He must have got out of the *wrong side of the bed*.

Getting out of the **wrong side of the bed** is an expression that began in ancient Rome. Like in the saying "set off on the wrong foot," (page 139) the Romans believed that the left side of anything, including the bed, was evil. They had a very real superstition that nefarious spirits lay on the left-hand side of the bed during the night. If someone was to get out of bed on that side, they would be forced to pass through those spirits, whose sinister ways would influence the person during the day, affecting their judgment and putting them in a bad mood. This negative influence would continue until the next morning, when the person got out of bed on the right.

Out of the Blue

MEANING: a complete and unexpected surprise

IN CONTEXT: I hadn't heard from her for years, then *out of the blue* she sent me an e-mail asking to meet up.

Out of the blue is a variation of the expression a bolt from the blue. The ancient Romans called a flash of lightning on a clear day a "thunderbolt from the blue." The blue in the phrase related to the blue of the sky. Lightning on a sunny day was obviously very rare, and the Romans began to use the saying to refer to any sudden surprise. It was first used in writing by Thomas Carlyle in his historical 1837 book *The French Revolution*, when he wrote, "Arrestment, sudden really as a bolt out of the blue, has hit strange victims."

Green with Envy

MEANING: to be very jealous; envious

IN CONTEXT: All my friends were *green with envy* when they saw my new car.

Green with envy began in ancient Greece. The Greeks believed that various illnesses and restless emotions, such as jealousy, were accompanied by an overproduction of bile, which lent a pallid green color to a person's complexion. In the 7th century, the Greek poet Sappho described a stricken lover as being green. But it was Shakespeare who popularized the expression in his 1603 play *Othello*, when he wrote, "Beware my lord of jealousy. It is the green-eyed monster which doth mock the meat it feeds on."

Achilles' Heel

MEANING: a weakness or vulnerability

IN CONTEXT: He was always so disciplined, except where alcohol was involved—that was his *Achilles' heel*.

Achilles' heel has its origins in an ancient Greek legend. Achilles was dipped into the river Styx by his mother Thetis in order to give him a skin of armor and make him invulnerable. But she held him by the heel, which did not get covered by water and thus remained a weak point. Achilles became a formidable warrior, but his arch enemy, Paris, discovered his weakness and killed him by shooting an arrow through Achilles' heel. This story was recounted by Homer in *The Iliad* in the 8th century BC, although it wasn't until the early 19th century that the phase came to mean what it does today.

Call a Spade a Spade

MEANING: to speak bluntly and describe something as it is

IN CONTEXT: I hated my friend's new book, so I decided to *call a spade a spade* and tell him up front.

Call a spade a spade originated with the ancient Greeks. The expression began with the comic playwright Menander when he wrote, "I call a fig a fig, a spade a spade." Some time later, the philosopher Plutarch wrote that the Macedonians were "a rude and clownish people who call a spade a spade." The phrase didn't enter the English language until 1542, when Nicholas Udall, the English playwright, translated part of the *Apophthegmatum opus* by Erasmus. The Greek word for "bowl" is similar to that of "spade," and it is now thought that the phrase may have been mistranslated and should actually be "call a bowl a bowl."

Go with the Flow

MEANING: to agree with the majority or do what the majority is doing

IN CONTEXT: I really didn't want to go to the nightclub but everyone else did, so I decided to *go with the flow*.

Despite popular belief, **go with the flow** did not begin in America during the free-spirited days of the late 1960s. Its origins lie in ancient Rome with the 2nd century emperor Marcus Aurelius. His reign was marked by much bloodshed—he defeated the Parthian Empire and won the Marcomannic Wars. But it was his intellectual thought and philosophical writings that defined him. His tome *Meditations*, which was written while expanding the Empire, describes how to find peace amid conflict by following nature as a source of inspiration and guidance. He likened time to a river of passing events that cannot be stopped, and suggested it was better to go with the flow than to fight against a strong current.

Spill the Beans

MEANING: divulge a secret or confess

IN CONTEXT: The witness was questioned extensively, and in the end he *spilled the beans* and told the court everything.

Spill the beans has its origins in ancient Greece. When an election was conducted for a new member to enter a secret society or private club, the existing members would vote. The members were given white and brown beans, and each member could only place one in a jar to cast his vote. A white bean meant "yes," and a brown bean meant "no." Nobody apart from the vote counters knew how many of each bean was in each jar, so the new member would never know just how popular or unpopular he was—unless, of course, the jar was knocked over. In that case, the beans would spill, and the votes would be divulged.

Purple Patch

MEANING: a period of notable success or good fortune

IN CONTEXT: Ryan had scored five touchdowns in his last three games; he was in a real *purple patch*.

Purple patch is an expression that stems from ancient Rome. At the height of the Roman Empire, purple (known as Tyrian or imperial purple) was a revered color and was reserved for emperors and other distinguished statesmen. This is because the purple dye was greatly prized and rare; it was obtained from the mucous secretions of predatory sea snails found in the Mediterranean Sea and it did not easily fade, but became brighter with weathering and sunlight. The Roman noblemen wore purple togas, and because they were considered exceptional people to whom all was provided, purple patch later became associated with success. During the 18th century it was often used in relation to overly florid literature, but by the 20th century it was applied to mean a period of good fortune.

It's All Greek to Me

MEANING: unable to understand something; something doesn't make any sense

IN CONTEXT: Darren studied the math text for hours but he couldn't make any sense of it. *It was all Greek to him.*

It's all Greek to me originates from the medieval Latin proverb "*Graecum est, non potest legi,*" which means "It is Greek, it cannot be read." The phrase was used by monk scribes at the time as they copied manuscripts in monastic libraries. Knowledge of the Greek language was dwindling and very few people could properly read it. The expression is yet another one that was brought into widespread usage by Shakespeare. His 1599 play *Julius Caesar* contains the line, "But, for mine own part, it was Greek to me."

Ears Are Burning

MEANING: one is being spoken about by people elsewhere

IN CONTEXT: When I walked into the room, Julia said, "Your *ears must have been burning*; we were just talking about you."

Often said as a person's **ears are burning**, this idiom originated with the ancient Romans. The Romans were very superstitious, and believed that different feelings in the body were signs of current or future events. It was said that a tingling, ringing, or burning feeling in the ears meant that the person was being talked about. The philosopher Pliny the Elder wrote in his book *Naturalis Historia* in AD 77, "It is acknowledged that the absent feel a presentiment of remarks about themselves by the ringing of their ears." The Romans also believed that everything on the left signified evil and the right signified good. It was held that if the left ear was burning, the speakers had malicious intent, and if the right ear was burning, the person was being praised.

Right-Hand Man

MEANING: an invaluable or indispensable assistant; second in command

IN CONTEXT: I'll give the job to Pete. He's my *right-hand man*.

Right-hand man has its origins in ancient Rome and Greece. In those times, leaders were often under threat of attack or assassination. Most people were right-handed, and so carried their swords on the right. It was from the right that an enemy could disable a man by grabbing his right arm (his sword arm), leaving him vulnerable to attack. With a trusted ally sitting on his right, the leader would be protected. The right-hand man was also in a position to disable the leader, so placing the man there was a great gesture of trust.

Rest on One's Laurels

MEANING: to be satisfied with one's past performance so as to think any future effort is unnecessary

IN CONTEXT: Stuart got straight As last year, so he thinks he doesn't have to study at all. He's really *resting on his laurels.*

To **rest on one's laurels** harks back to ancient Greece. Apollo, the famous Greek god, was usually depicted with a crown of laurel leaves around his head. A wreath of laurels became a symbol of status and achievement, and these wreaths were presented to winning athletes at the Pythian Games, which were held every four years from the 6th century BC. The Romans then embraced the laurel as a status symbol and would present wreaths to victorious generals. Those who were presented with such wreaths became known as "laureates," a term that is used to this day. Because they were then so respected, laureates were able to bask in the glory of their achievements and rest on their laurels. It was only later that the phrase developed negative connotations.

Lick It into Shape

MEANING: to mold something or someone to suit a situation

IN CONTEXT: The fight was only four weeks away and the boxer was unfit, so his coach had to *lick him into shape.*

To **lick it into shape** derives from the ancient Roman belief that animals were born formless and their mothers had to lick them into the required shape. This idea probably arose because all mammals are born covered with thick afterbirth, which can make them unrecognizable. The mother then licks that off and the properly formed animal "appears." Bear cubs, in particular, are born in a seemingly shapeless form and receive a lot of attention from their mothers, so this would have also lent weight to the Romans' belief.

To Have a Frog in Your Throat

MEANING: a feeling of hoarseness; a lump in one's throat, especially through fear

IN CONTEXT: I always *get a frog in my throat* when I'm about to do a speech.

To have a frog in your throat began in ancient times. Many years ago, clean drinking water was not readily available and people drank water gathered from ponds or streams. A superstition (and in some cases a genuine fear) arose, that accidentally swallowing the eggs of a frog would lead to tadpoles hatching in the stomach. A tadpole would then form into a frog, which would try to escape through the person's mouth, producing a choking feeling as it did. The expression was being used figuratively in America by the mid-1800s.

At Bay

MEANING: to fend off or keep at a distance

IN CONTEXT: I felt like I was about to get a cold but I took some extra vitamins, which seemed to keep it *at bay*.

Many believe that to keep something **at bay** derives from the idea of holding off baying hounds from a fox. However, this origin only dates back to the 1300s, while the phrase actually began with the ancient Romans and Greeks. They believed that the bay tree had protective powers because it never seemed to be struck by lightning. Because of this, people at the time would take shelter under the trees during storms. Soldiers also started wearing bay leaves on their heads as protection during thunderstorms. They believed the leaves would keep the lightning at bay and would also shield them from the enemy. The supposed power of the bay leaf spread, and during the Great Plague of London in 1665, many citizens wore bay leaves in an attempt to keep the disease at bay.

Red-Letter Day

MEANING: an important or significant day

IN CONTEXT: Winning the trophy for the first time was a real *red-letter day* for our team.

Red-letter day originated in ancient Rome. During the Roman Republic, which began in 509 BC, important days were indicated in red on calendars. By the 15th century, medieval church calendars also had religious holidays, saints' days, and festivals in red ink, while the other days were written in black. These days became known as red-letter days, and many calendars today still use the practice. In a number of countries, including Norway, Denmark, Sweden, and South Korea, a public holiday is called a "red day" for this reason.

Taken with a Pinch of Salt

MEANING: with a healthy dose of suspicion or caution

IN CONTEXT: Dianne has been known to stretch the truth at times. *Take what she says with a pinch of salt.*

Also said as a "grain" of salt, **taken with a pinch of salt** owes its origins to ancient Rome. The philosopher Pliny the Elder wrote the story of King Mithridates VI of Pontus in his book *Naturalis Historia* in AD 77. The King had built up his immunity to poison by regularly ingesting small doses of a poison recipe—two dried walnuts, two figs, and twenty leaves of rue, all ground together. Addito salis grano, Pliny recounted, "add a grain of salt," to make the mixture more palatable and easier to swallow. It is not known when the expression changed to mean what it does today.

Hanging by a Thread

MEANING: something is ready to fall apart or could change in an instant

IN CONTEXT: The President was facing a vote of no confidence, and his leadership was really *hanging by a thread.*

Hanging by a thread originated from a banquet held in 400 BC by Dionysius the Elder, the tyrant King of ancient Syracuse, for Damocles, one of his courtiers. King Dionysius had become annoyed with Damocles' constant flattery and invited him to the banquet. A sword was hung by the ceiling, suspended by a single hair. Damocles was required to sit beneath it to remind him of his tenuous position in the court. Both the sword, and Damocles' life, were hanging by a thread.

Give the Thumbs Up

MEANING: to give acceptance or approval of something

IN CONTEXT: The film was excellent and we all *gave it the thumbs up*.

Used throughout the world as a gesture of approval, **give the thumbs up** dates back to the gladiatorial contests in ancient Rome. In the amphitheaters of Rome 2,000 years ago, a victorious gladiator would look to the emperor to determine whether to spare his opponent. If the crowd were shouting "mitte, mitte" (meaning "let him go free") in appreciation of the loser's fighting skills and bravery, the emperor would give a thumbs up gesture and the defeated man would be spared. But if the crowd shouted "lugula" and the emperor gave a thumbs down signal, he would be killed. The expression became widespread in 1872 with *Pollice Verso*, a painting by the French artist Jean-Léon Gérôme, which depicts the "thumbs down" gesture at the end of a Colosseum battle.

The Die Is Cast

MEANING: something is past the point of no return; an irrevocable choice has been made

IN CONTEXT: The senator's speech about health-care reform meant there was no turning back on the issue. *The die had been cast.*

The die is cast is another expression that originated in ancient Greece and Rome. A die is one of a pair of playing dice, and to cast means to throw. The phrase actually began in around 300 BC with the Greek dramatist Menander. It was a proverb that was discovered in his play *Arrhephoros*, used in relation to a game of dice and meaning that once the die was cast, the players had no choice but to accept the outcome. The expression was made famous by Julius Caesar in 49 BC. "Let the die be cast," he said as he led his army across the Rubicon River into Rome, committing them to a civil war.

No Stone Unturned

MEANING: to make every possible effort

IN CONTEXT: The detective promised to leave *no stone unturned* in his hunt for the killer.

Arguably the oldest expression that we have, **no stone unturned** comes from ancient Greece. In 477 BC the Greeks, led by Polycrates, defeated the Persians in the Battle of Plataea. It was rumored at the time that Mardonius, the Persian general, had buried a large treasure in his tent after the defeat. Unable to find the treasure, Polycrates consulted the Oracle of Delphi, who advised him to "move every stone" in his search. Polycrates redoubled his efforts and found the treasure. The phrase was popularized when the Greek playwright Euripides wrote it as "leave no stone unturned."

Not Worth His Salt

MEANING: to be ineffective or not deserving of one's pay

IN CONTEXT: Mark's a very lazy man and has no stamina. He's really *not worth his salt*.

Not worth his salt derives from Roman times. Before the invention of canned goods and refrigeration, salt was a valuable commodity in the preservation of food. Roman soldiers received some of their wages as an allowance of salt. This was known as a "salarium", which takes its root from *sal*, the Latin word for "salt"—our modern word "salary" actually derives from it. If a soldier did not perform well and was not up to scratch, it was said that he was not worth his salt.

Dog Day Afternoon

MEANING: a hot afternoon that makes a person lazy

IN CONTEXT: It was a *dog day afternoon*, so we just lazed in the pool.

Dog day afternoon owes its origins to ancient Roman astronomy. The Romans called the days between July 3 and August 11 the Canicularis Dies, or Dog Days. This is when Sirius, the dog star, rises and sets in line with the sun in the northern hemisphere. These were usually the hottest days of the year, and the Romans believed that this was caused by the combined heat of the dog star and the sun.

Lily Livered

MEANING: a coward or cowardly behavior

IN CONTEXT: The young boy ran away from the bully who accused him of being a *lily livered* coward.

Lily livered is yet another expression that we owe to the ancient Greeks. They believed that the liver was the organ that created blood, and that a poorly functioning liver resulted in physical and mental weakness. In line with this belief, they thought that a pale, lily-colored complexion indicated a cowardly person, while rosy cheeks would be found on a strong man in good health. The Greeks also had the custom of sacrificing an animal before each battle. They looked to the animal's liver as an omen—a liver full of blood was a good sign, but a pale liver did not augur well. Shakespeare brought the phrase to the mainstream when he used it in his 1606 play *Macbeth*.

Burn Your Bridges

MEANING: to put yourself in a position from which there is no return

IN CONTEXT: Luke left his job on good terms, as he didn't want to *burn his bridges*.

Often used in the negative form with "don't," **burn your bridges** dates back to ancient Roman times. When Roman armies crossed a river to invade a new territory, the general in command would order the bridge they had crossed to be burned. This ensured the soldiers couldn't have second thoughts and retreat. They were forced to fight for their lives. The territories being invaded sometimes used the same technique, burning their bridges as they retreated so that the Romans could not follow. They were even known to burn their own towns so the Romans had no shelter or food when they arrived.

Set Off on the Wrong Foot

MEANING: to make a bad start to a relationship or project

IN CONTEXT: We *set off on the wrong foot* and failed to get approval for the project.

Set off on the wrong foot dates back to ancient Rome. The Romans were very superstitious about anything on the left. They believed the left was evil and, in fact, the Latin word for left is *sinister*. Gaius Petronius was a Roman courtier and adviser to Emperor Nero in the 1st century, and he had a particular aversion to anything left-sided. Petronius made an order that no Roman should enter or leave a building by the left foot. He even had guards placed at the entrances to public buildings to ensure the order was adhered to. But not much enforcement was needed, as most Romans agreed that to go against the ruling was to flirt with disaster. They rarely set off on the wrong foot.

Eat Your Heart Out

MEANING: to feel sorrow or longing; a good-humored taunt to someone

IN CONTEXT: "*Eat your heart out*, John," said Robin. "You had your chance and now I'm seeing someone else."

Eat your heart out originated in ancient Greece over 2,500 years ago. It stems from Greek mythology and the story of Bellerophon, the great slayer of monsters, who was depicted as eating his heart in grief when the gods Ares and Artemis killed his children. This was described by Homer in his classical text *The Iliad*. The Greeks believed the heart to be the emotional center of the body, which is the likely reason it would be eaten in times of sorrow. The Greek biographer Diogenes Laertius later credited Pythagoras with saying, "Do not eat your heart," warning against wasting one's life by worrying about something.

Fits to a T

MEANING: it fits precisely; to be very appropriate

IN CONTEXT: Brad was a strong man, so the digging job *fitted him to a T*.

The expression **fits to a T** derives from medieval Latin. The "T" in the phrase stands for tittle, which comes from the Latin word *titulus*, meaning "tiny." A tittle is a small stroke or point in writing or printing. Originally "fits to a tittle," the expression was first used by the English theologian John Wycliffe in the 1300s to refer to the very minor differences in his version of the New Testament.

The Wrong End of the Stick

MEANING: to misunderstand a situation entirely

IN CONTEXT: John was seen walking along with Anita, but his girlfriend got *the wrong end of the stick* and thought he had been cheating.

The wrong end of the stick began with the toilet habits of ancient Rome. The Romans used communal toilets where people sat side by side and discussed the day's events. Toilet paper was not yet invented, so to address personal hygiene issues, a cloth or sponge was tied to one end of a short staff, which was passed from person to person. It was important to pay close attention when picking up or being passed the implement, because nobody wanted to get the wrong end of the stick.

Mountain Out of a Molehill

MEANING: to exaggerate something out of all proportion

IN CONTEXT: Anna dropped her burger and started crying hysterically. She always makes a *mountain out of a molehill*.

Mountain out of a molehill owes its origins to ancient Greece. The original expression was "make an elephant out of a fly," which was an old Latin proverb used at the time. In 1548, Nicholas Udall, the English playwright, did a translation  in his work *Paraphrase of Erasmus*, which included the line "The Sophistes of Greece could through their copiousness make an elephant of a fly and a mountain of a molehill." Erasmus had included the "elephant of a fly" reference in his original work, but Udall added mountain out of a molehill, and the phrase has continued ever since.

By Heart

MEANING: to know or memorize something perfectly

IN CONTEXT: I had studied so hard for the exam that I knew the material *by heart*.

By heart dates back to ancient Greece. In the 4th century BC, the great philosopher Aristotle believed that the heart was the intelligence center of the body. He held that the heart governed human emotions because of the fluttering that people experienced, and that it was also responsible for thinking and memory. If something was studied, it was committed to the heart. The word "record" actually comes from the Latin words *re*, meaning "again," and *cor*, meaning "heart." So if something was recorded in the memory, it was learned by heart.

Lap of the Gods

MEANING: a situation whose outcome is unclear and can't be influenced

IN CONTEXT: The doctors have done all they can, so whether he survives or not is in the *lap of the gods*.

Some say the expression **lap of the gods** began with the practice of leaving gifts of thanks with statues of gods. While this has occurred for centuries, the phrase derives from *The Iliad*, Homer's text from the 8th century BC. In the story, Achilles battles the Trojans and kills Hector's brother Polydorus. Hector sees this and challenges Achilles, brandishing a spear in his face. "I know you are brave and stronger than me by far," says Hector to Achilles. "But these things lie in the lap of the gods. Though I'm the weaker man, I'll take your life." Achilles survives, and the Trojans are defeated.

CHAPTER 8
Bold as Brass:
People and Names

To Plug Something

MEANING: to promote something

IN CONTEXT: The radio DJ was really *plugging* the new song. He played it three times a day.

To plug something owes its beginnings to Captain Leonard Frank Plugge, a British businessman and politician who was prominent in the early 1900s. Plugge created a broadcasting company that bought airtime from European radio stations. He reached an agreement with the French station, Radio Normandy, to broadcast programs and transmit them to England. Plugge partially financed Radio Normandy by receiving payments to play and promote records. It was from this practice and Plugge's name that the expression was born.

Blue Blood

MEANING: a member of a socially prominent and wealthy family

IN CONTEXT: The Johnsons have got a lot of money and have been in the area for generations. They're real *blue bloods*.

Blue blood is a translation of the Spanish *sangre azul*, and relates to aristocrats who lived in Castile. From their invasion in the 8th century, the Moors, who were from North Africa and had dark skin, ruled over much of Spain. Many interracial marriages took place, but the oldest and proudest families from Castile were quick to boast that they had never intermarried with the Moors or any other race. As a result, they were pure and remained extremely fair skinned, making their veins appear a profoundly blue color against their white skin. They took this to be a mark of good breeding and called themselves the *sangre azul*—the blue bloods. This was later used in England to describe the nobility.

Your Name Is Mud

MEANING: a person who is unpopular or out of favor

IN CONTEXT: Young Ronnie was caught stealing lunch money at school, and now *his name is mud*.

Unrelated to wet soil, **your name is mud** should actually read "Mudd." In 1865, John Wilkes Booth assassinated President Abraham Lincoln by shooting him in the Ford Theater in Washington DC. Booth broke his leg while escaping and managed to ride his horse to the house of Dr. Samuel Mudd. Dr. Mudd was ignorant of the grave events that had just unfolded and provided Booth with medical assistance. Mudd learned of the shooting the next day and contacted police. He was arrested, convicted of conspiracy to murder, and sentenced to life in jail. Mudd was pardoned and released in 1869, but the public never forgave him and his name was forever tarnished.

Bold As Brass

MEANING: with extreme confidence, without regard to consequences

IN CONTEXT: Candace is as *bold as brass*. There were a lot of people at the beach, but she just stripped off naked and got in the water.

Bold as brass relates to a man named Brass Crosby, a London magistrate in the 1770s. At that time in England, the publication of parliamentary debates was considered a breach of privilege and was illegal. When two London printers published reports on parliament, they were arrested and brought before the court. Disagreeing with the law, Crosby freed them. As a result, he was then committed to jail for treason. By the time of his release, he had become famous because of his bold stand of defiance.

Peeping Tom

MEANING: a man who secretly observes naked women or sexual acts for his own gratification

IN CONTEXT: There was a furor at the gym when a *peeping Tom* was caught outside the ladies' locker room window.

Peeping Tom has its origins with the story of Lady Godiva. In the 11th century, Godiva was married to Leofric, the Earl of Mercia, who owned large landholdings. He imposed heavy taxes on the less wealthy, which resulted in public outrage. Godiva disagreed with the taxes and implored her husband to reduce them. Thinking she would never do it, Leofric agreed to lower the taxes on the condition that Godiva rode a horse naked through the streets of Coventry in England. She decided to take up the challenge, and as a mark of respect the townsfolk agreed to stay indoors, close their shutters, and not watch the highly publicized spectacle. Everyone kept their word except for the tailor in the town, Tom. Tom was unable to resist a glimpse of the nubile Godiva and peeped through his shutters.

The Real McCoy

MEANING: an authentic or genuine person or thing; not a substitute

IN CONTEXT: The sculpture was not a reproduction. It was *the real McCoy*.

The real McCoy is an expression with a number of potential origins which have often been hotly contested. The most cogent theory is that it derives from "Kid McCoy," the name used by Norman Selby, the American welterweight boxer who dominated the sport and was at the height of his fame in the 1890s. McCoy had many imitators who would use his name in an attempt to capitalize on his popularity. It became so commonplace for Kid McCoy imposters at fairground boxing rings around the country to challenge the locals for money, that few people ever believed it was actually him. Years after he had retired, McCoy was in a bar when he was challenged by a drunk who was much larger he. The drunk's friends warned him not to fight McCoy, but the drunk didn't believe it was really him. Provoked to his limit, McCoy knocked the man out with a single blow. When he came to, the drunk admitted, "You're right, he is the real McCoy."

A Place in the Sun

MEANING: an enjoyable holiday destination or holiday home; an imaginary place of nirvana

IN CONTEXT: We had saved for years and could finally afford *a place in the sun*.

A place in the sun has its unexpected origins in Europe's colonization of "uncivilized continents" in the 19th century.

Known as the "Scramble for Africa," a number of European countries sought to expand their empire, and Germany was no exception. Kaiser Wilhelm II's foreign policy called Weltpolitik aimed to transform Germany into a global power through the development of a large navy and the acquisition of overseas colonies. The policy was debated in the Reichstag on December 6, 1897, and in that seminal discussion, German Foreign Secretary Bernhard von Bulow said, "We wish to throw no one into the shade, but we demand our own place in the sun." The expression quickly grew from there to mean what it does today.

Cock and Bull Story

MEANING: a fabricated or exaggerated story

IN CONTEXT: Michelle told us she'd studied for thirty hours straight, but it was obviously a *cock and bull story*.

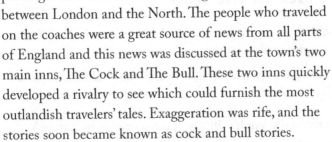

Cock and bull story has its origins with the town of Stony Stratford in Buckinghamshire, England. In the height of the coach-travel era of the 18th and 19th centuries, Stony Stratford was an important stopping-off point for passenger and mail coaches traveling between London and the North. The people who traveled on the coaches were a great source of news from all parts of England and this news was discussed at the town's two main inns, The Cock and The Bull. These two inns quickly developed a rivalry to see which could furnish the most outlandish travelers' tales. Exaggeration was rife, and the stories soon became known as cock and bull stories.

Spruce Up

MEANING: to tidy up and make stylish

IN CONTEXT: He was having guests to his house so he decided to *spruce it up* a little.

To **spruce up** has curious origins. "Spruce" is a 14th-century word that is a variant of "Pruce," which was a shortened version of the name Prussia. Prussia was a state in northern Europe that met its end shortly after World War II. During its early days, things imported from Prussia were referred to as spruce and considered high quality. Spruce leather was of a particularly top grade and was often said to be "smart." This aided the expression's transformation to its current meaning by the 16th century.

Fifteen Minutes of Fame

MEANING: a brief period of celebrity or media publicity

IN CONTEXT: Joelle made a bold announcement at the directors' meeting and got her *fifteen minutes of fame.*

The phrase **fifteen minutes of fame** was first coined by the American artist Andy Warhol. In the catalogue for a 1968 exhibition of his work at the Moderna Museet gallery in Stockholm, Sweden, he included the words, "In the future, everybody will be world famous for fifteen minutes." While Warhol is widely credited with the expression, a photographer named Nat Finkelstein claims he first said it when working with the artist in 1966. A crowd had gathered and was trying to get into the photos being taken of Warhol, who remarked that everybody wants to be famous. "Yeah," Finkelstein replied, "for about fifteen minutes, Andy."

However, Warhol maintained that he was responsible for the phrase and in 1979 he repeated it, claiming that the line had a sound basis.

Smart Alec

MEANING: a wise guy or know-it-all

IN CONTEXT: Sam thought he knew everything and he was always ready with a witty comment. He was a real *smart Alec*.

Smart Alec dates back to the 1840s in New York to a man named Alec Hoag. Hoag was a fraudster and a con man. Working in cahoots with his wife Miranda, he would have her pose as a prostitute to lure in unwary customers. Once the customer was in a compromising situation with his wife, Hoag would sneak in and steal anything of value from the victim. Hoag was caught doing this on a number of occasions, but escaped arrest by bribing police officers. But Hoag pushed his luck too far in one instance, and decided not to pay the police their cut. He was sentenced to jail, and the New York police began calling any criminal who was a little too clever for his own good a smart Alec.

Jack the Lad

MEANING: a brash and carefree young man

IN CONTEXT: I don't want you going out with him. He's a bad influence, a real *Jack the lad*.

The expression **Jack the lad** owes its beginnings to Jack Sheppard, a twenty-two year old man born in London in 1702. Sheppard was a notorious and reckless thief whose antics made him a household name throughout England. He was caught and imprisoned five times, escaping four times through ingenious means—he sawed through the roof of his cell on one occasion and on another, he picked the locks of his shackles using his finger nail. Jack became a popular hero who inspired a number of songs and plays. During his final stay in jail in 1724, he was guarded day and night and then hanged at Tyburn in front of a crowd of over 200,000.

Run Amok

MEANING: engage in wild or erratic behavior

IN CONTEXT: The men were drunk and they started smashing bottles and really *running amok*.

Run amok dates from 16th-century Malaysia. The Amuco were a band of Javanese and Malay warriors. They believed that warriors who died in victorious battles became favorites with the gods, while warriors that failed were dishonored and killed. This led the men to fight with extreme frenzy and violence. Their seeming desire for indiscriminate and unrestrained violence fascinated the European explorers of the 18th century. Captain James Cook detailed an account of the Amuco in his 1772 Voyages when he wrote, "To run amock is to get drunk with opium…to sally forth from the house, kill the person or persons supposed to have injured the Amock, and any other person that attempts to impede his passage." Amok officially became a psychiatric medical condition in 1849 and is still considered one today.

Air Your Dirty Laundry in Public

MEANING: talk to others in public about private matters

IN CONTEXT: I was taught not to *air my dirty laundry in public*, so I only discuss private things at home.

Sometimes used with "wash" instead of "air" and "linen" instead of "laundry," **air your dirty laundry in public** owes its beginnings to Napoleon Bonaparte. Napoleon was exiled  to the island of Elba in 1814 after he was forced to abdicate from the French throne. He was made emperor of the island and allowed an army of 700 men. Despite the island being surrounded by the British navy, Napoleon managed to escape on a boat after less than a year there. Back in France he was asked about his experiences in exile. "It is at home and not in public that one washes one's dirty linen," he replied.

John Hancock

MEANING: a signature

IN CONTEXT: If you put your *John Hancock* here, the deal will be formal.

John Hancock was an American merchant and statesman who lived from 1737 to 1793. He was the Governor of Massachusetts and president of the Second Continental Congress. Hancock was one of the men to sign the American Declaration of Independence in 1776. His flamboyant signature is the largest on the document and is nearly five inches long. Because of that, his name became synonymous for any signature. It is told that when he signed the document he said, "There—I guess King George or John Bull will be able to read that without his spectacles."

Barking Mad

MEANING: crazy

IN CONTEXT: By the end of a weekend drinking in the sun, we had all gone *barking mad*.

Barking mad does not relate to the obvious analogy of comparing an insane person to a crazed dog. It is often disputed, but its likely origins actually lie in the east London suburban town of Barking. In medieval times, Barking was home to a lunatic asylum. The asylum was notorious for its particularly deranged inhabitants. It wasn't long before the expression barking mad was used throughout England to refer to someone who would not be out of place there.

Nosy Parker

MEANING: a nosy, prying person

IN CONTEXT: We tried to keep our voices down because Mrs. Archer next door was a real *nosy Parker* and loved any form of gossip.

Nosy Parker began in the 16th century and is named after Matthew Parker, the Archbishop of Canterbury who served under Elizabeth I. Parker was a forerunner in church reform and sought to obtain a detailed account of the qualifications and activities of the clergy. To this end, he ordered a number of inquiries, which were met with much derision from those answerable to him. This reputation earned him the nickname "Nosy," because it was said that he was always sticking his nose in and trying to sniff things out. Nosy Parker had become a popular expression by the late 19th century.

Mickey Finn

MEANING: a drug slipped into someone's drink surreptitiously

IN CONTEXT: I'd only had two drinks but I was almost on the floor. Someone must have slipped me a *Mickey Finn*.

Often referred to as "slipping someone a Mickey," the expression **Mickey Finn** originated on South State Street, Chicago, in the late 19th century. Mickey Finn was the manager of the Palm Garden Restaurant and the Lone Star Saloon. Finn was an unscrupulous low-life and was known to lace his customer's drinks with knock-out drops (containing chloral hydrate), causing them to become incapacitated so he could then rob them. The authorities got wind of Finn's illicit practices. Finn escaped jail, but in 1903 the bars were closed down. One newspaper headline described the event: "Mickey Finn's alleged 'knock-out drops' put him out of business."

CHAPTER 9
In the Doghouse: Literature

World Is Your Oyster

MEANING: you can do or achieve anything you like; the world is yours to enjoy

IN CONTEXT: If you can just finish your law degree, the *world is your oyster*.

The **world is your oyster** is a Shakespearean expression. It began with his 1602 play *The Merry Wives of Windsor*. In a conversation between two of the characters,  Falstaff and Pistol, Falstaff says, "I will not lend thee a penny." "Why then, the world's mine oyster," replies Pistol, "which I with sword shall open." The metaphoric implication is that Pistol is going to use his sword to open an oyster to get to the pearl inside and have his fortune.

Add Insult to Injury

MEANING: an action or comment that makes an already-bad situation even worse

IN CONTEXT: After losing his job, Nick's severance pay was also cut, which *added insult to injury*.

To **add insult to injury** dates back to 25 BC and is derived from the fables of Phaedrus, a writer in ancient Rome. He told the story of The Bald Man and the Fly, in which a fly stings a bald man on top of his head. The man swats at the fly, attempting to kill it, but the fly moves away and the man hits himself on the head instead. The man not only gets bitten, but he makes it worse by hitting his head. "You wished to kill me for a touch," the fly says. "What will you do to yourself since you have added insult to injury?" The phrase had passed into English by the mid-1700s.

Artful Dodger

MEANING: a rogue who avoids getting into trouble for his crimes through devious means

IN CONTEXT: Jake was responsible for the graffiti but he convinced the teacher he didn't do it. That boy is a real *artful dodger*.

Artful dodger derives from the Charles Dickens novel *Oliver Twist*. Published in 1838, the novel was met with immediate critical and popular acclaim. One of the characters in the book is Jack Dawkins, a cunning pickpocket and member of Fagin's gang of thieves. As part of the story, Dickens nicknames Dawkins the Artful Dodger, and the expression has been used from that time to describe any wily ruffian.

The Lion's Share

MEANING: the largest part of something

IN CONTEXT: We had done the same amount of work for the presentation, but Courtney took *the lion's share* of the credit because she is so outgoing.

The lion's share derives from one of Aesop's fables, which now bears that name. It tells the story of a lion, a fox, a wolf, and an ass who kill a stag to eat. The bounty is divided into quarters to share equally, but before they start eating, the lion claims the first portion because he is the king of the jungle. He then claims the second portion because he is the strongest, then the third portion because he is the most courageous. The other animals are left with the last quarter to eat, but they are too afraid to claim it with the lion standing over them. So depending on the version of the story, the lion's share is either three quarters, or everything.

Clutching at Straws

MEANING: to try any method to help a situation, even if success is unlikely

IN CONTEXT: She's hoping the new herbal treatment will help her illness, but I think she's *clutching at straws*.

Sometimes said with "grasping," **clutching at straws** originated with the English philosopher Sir Thomas More, who was beheaded for refusing to acknowledge King Henry VIII as the Supreme Head of the Church of England. While awaiting his execution, More wrote *Dialogue of Comfort Against Tribulation*. Published in 1534, the book is a fictional account of More's life. In it he writes that "a man in peril of drowning catchest whatsoever cometh next to hand…be it never so simple a stick." By the 19th century the expression had developed from "catch" and "stick" to clutching at straws.

Ivory Tower

MEANING: an attitude of sheltered retreat, remote from the real world and everyday affairs

IN CONTEXT: Having been an academic for years and living in an *ivory tower*, Joe couldn't handle his practical role in the new company.

To live in an **ivory tower** has its origins in the world of literature. As with a number of other expressions, it has French beginnings and derives from a poem called "Pensees d'Août" ("Thoughts of August"). This was written in 1837 by the critic Charles Sainte-Beuve and is about a man named Alfred de Vigny. De Vigny was a poet who lived a withdrawn and sheltered life away from the harsh realities of the world. Sainte-Beuve describes de Vigny's life as isolated, writing that he lived in a secluded *tour d'ivoire*, which translates to ivory tower. The phrase came to apply to intellectuals and academics who were thought to be removed from the real world.

Go the Whole Hog

MEANING: to do something entirely without reservation; to hold back nothing

IN CONTEXT: If you can afford to build such an expensive house, you might as well *go the whole hog* and get a swimming pool as well.

Go the whole hog was first recorded by the Englishman William Cowper in his 1779 poem "The Love of the World Reproved; or Hypocrisy Detested." The poem mocks Muslims over their supposed ambiguity on the restrictions against eating pork. In it, Cowper mocks them, suggesting that while sampling each part of the pig to test which is not permissible to eat, the whole hog is eaten: "But for one piece they thought it hard, from the whole hog to be debarred." The expression entered the mainstream with 18th-century meat vendors in America. Butchers offered meat for sale by the pound, but a discounted rate was charged if the whole animal was purchased. Andrew Jackson then used the phrase as a slogan in his 1828 presidential campaign, which he eventually won, to refer to "going all the way."

All Hell Broke Loose

MEANING: wild and erratic things occurred

IN CONTEXT: When the teacher left the classroom for ten minutes *all hell broke loose*.

All hell broke loose has literary origins. The expression comes from John Milton's epic poem *Paradise Lost*. Published in ten volumes in 1667, the poem tells the biblical tale of the Garden of Eden. In one part, just before he casts him out of the Garden, the angel Gabriel asks Satan why he had traveled alone and hadn't been joined by the other inhabitants of Hell. Gabriel poses the question as, "Wherefore with thee came not all hell broke loose?"

In the Doghouse

MEANING: disgraced and out of favor, usually a husband with a wife

IN CONTEXT: I was *in the doghouse* because I'd been out drinking until late the night before.

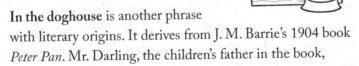

In the doghouse is another phrase with literary origins. It derives from J. M. Barrie's 1904 book *Peter Pan*. Mr. Darling, the children's father in the book, inadvertently prevents Nana, the family dog, from protecting the children by tying her up outside. This allows Peter Pan to lure the children away to Neverland. Mr. Darling blames himself for their disappearance, and as a punishment for his behavior, consigns himself to live in the doghouse until the children return. *Peter Pan* was a very popular book and, as a result, the expression quickly came into widespread usage.

Sour Grapes

MEANING: acting in a jealous way after a disappointment

IN CONTEXT: She was desperate to make the team, but when she didn't, she had *sour grapes* and pretended like she didn't care.

Sour grapes is one of a number of expressions attributed to Aesop, the ancient Greek writer. In his fable "The Fox and the Grapes," a hungry fox sees some ripe grapes hanging from a trellised vine. The fox uses all of its cunning to get at them, but eventually tires and is unsuccessful. Knowing that it won't be able to get the grapes, the embittered fox says that it didn't really want them anyway, declaring, "the grapes are sour and not ripe as I thought."

Blowing Hot and Cold

MEANING: to change one's mind; be inconsistent

IN CONTEXT: Mike keeps talking about building a new house but he's *blowing hot and cold* on the topic.

Blowing hot and cold derives from classical mythology. It comes from another of the fables of Aesop. It tells the story of a man who meets a satyr (a mythical beast that is part-man and part-goat) on a winter's day. At first the man blew on his hands to warm them up. The satyr then invited the man to his house and gave him some porridge. The man blew on the porridge to cool it down. The satyr was aghast. "Out you go," he said. "I will have naught to do with a man who can blow hot and cold with the same breath." The expression was being used figuratively by the 17th century. The controversial English churchman, William Chillingworth, referred to the phrase in his 1638 book *The Religion of Protestants* when he wrote, "These men can blow hot and cold out of the same mouth to serve several purposes."

Cold Feet

MEANING: a loss of nerve, or doubts about a situation

IN CONTEXT: They had been engaged for two years, but on the wedding day the groom got *cold feet* and didn't show up.

Often used in relation to marriage, **cold feet** has literary beginnings. It is thought to have been first used in the 1862 novel *Seed-Time and Harvest* by the German writer Fritz Reuter. In that book, a card player on a bad streak is fearful of losing all his money. Instead of conceding defeat and walking away with dignity, he withdraws from the game claiming that his feet are cold, making him unable to concentrate. The phrase eventually came to mean backing out of any situation through a loss of nerve.

Dark Horse

MEANING: a competitor that is unknown or wins unexpectedly

IN CONTEXT: I never thought Kenny had it in him to run a marathon. He's a real *dark horse*.

The expression **dark horse** originated with Benjamin Disraeli, the 19th-century British politician and writer who twice became Prime Minister. In his 1831 novel *The Young Duke*, Disraeli describes a horse race where the two favorites are beaten by a rank outsider. "A dark horse, which had never been thought of, rushed past the grand stand in sweeping triumph." It was common in the racing industry at the time for owners to conceal their fastest horses until the day of the race, and because of Disraeli's book, they became known as dark horses. The figurative usage soon followed.

Between You, Me, and the Lamppost

MEANING: a secret between two people

IN CONTEXT: *Between you, me, and the lamppost*, Matt is going to get fired tomorrow.

Between you, me, and the lamppost is yet another expression that stems from the 19th century and the British writer Charles Dickens. The lamppost in the saying represents the epitome of deafness, making clear that apart from the two people concerned, nobody else can know the information. It was first used by Dickens in his 1838 book *Nicholas Nickleby*.

Leap of Faith

MEANING: a trust in the unknown where the outcome can't be predicted

IN CONTEXT: I allowed the carpenter to build my house without having any plans. It required a *leap of faith* on my part.

Leap of faith has literary origins and began as a "great leap in the dark." Thomas Hobbes of Malmesbury was an English philosopher who suffered a stroke and died in 1679. His final words were, "Now I am about to take my last voyage, a great leap in the dark." A few years later, in 1697, Sir John Vanbrugh wrote the comedy *The Provoked Wife*. It contained the line "Now I am for Hobbes' voyage, a great leap in the dark." It was this reference that popularized the expression, which was then quoted by many other writers before it changed into a leap of faith to describe any uncertainty.

Big Brother Is Watching

MEANING: one's actions are being monitored by the authorities

IN CONTEXT: You have to be careful what you search for on the internet these days, as *Big Brother is always watching*.

Big brother is watching has become a commonplace expression in recent years because of the popular reality television show. The phrase was born in 1949 with George Orwell's novel *Nineteen Eighty-Four*. Big Brother is

the leader of a totalitarian state in the book, where every citizen is under continual surveillance by the government. Telescreens are used to monitor the people, who are reminded of this by the slogan "Big Brother is watching you" being on constant display.

Eat Me Out of House and Home

MEANING: to eat everything that someone has in the house

IN CONTEXT: That huge dog is *eating me out of house and home*.

Eat me out of house and home is another expression coined by the great bard William Shakespeare. In his historical play *Henry IV, Part 2*, written in 1599, one of the characters, Mistress Quickly, drags the rotund Sir John Falstaff before the court to seek compensation. In making her case she says, "It is more than for some, my lord; it is for all, all I have. He hath eaten me out of house and home; he hath put all my substance into that fat belly of his: but I will have some of it out again, or I will ride thee o'nights like the mare."

As Sure As Eggs

MEANING: used to describe an absolute certainty

IN CONTEXT: *As sure as eggs*, she'll be back here asking for more money tomorrow.

As sure as eggs is a contraction of the longer expression "as sure as eggs is eggs." It is a corruption of the logical mathematical formula "$x = x$," and is purposely grammatically incorrect: the phrase should read "as sure as eggs are eggs." It is not known how "$x = x$" became "eggs is eggs," but Charles

Dickens used the phrase in his 1837 book *The Pickwick Papers*, and it became a popular expression from that time.

Catch-22

MEANING: a "no-win" situation; an impossible dilemma

IN CONTEXT: Professional bull riding is a *catch-22*. You have to stay on for eight seconds, but the bull has to be so aggressive that it's almost impossible to ride for that long.

Catch-22 originated with the 1961 book of that name by Joseph Heller. Set on a US air force base during World War II, the pilots were desperate to be exempted from flying any more dangerous missions. The catch was that the pilots must be mad to fly another mission, but by applying for an exemption on the grounds of insanity, the applicant proved himself to be sane. Either way he had to continue flying. The title began as Catch-18 and went through various different numbers before Heller settled on *Catch-22*. The phrase quickly came to mean any impossible dilemma or paradoxical situation.

Dropping like Flies

MEANING: falling down ill or dead in large numbers; a swift decline in numbers

IN CONTEXT: Five employees were off sick in the last week. They're really *dropping like flies*.

Dropping like flies has its origins with "The Brave Little Tailor," a German fairy tale by the Brothers Grimm. Dating from 1640, it tells the story of a tailor who is preparing to eat some jam. When flies land on his food, he kills seven of them with one blow of his hand. He makes a belt celebrating his achievement and puts the words "Seven at One Blow" on it. Inspired by this, he sets out to seek his fortune. While the phrase doesn't actually appear in the text, the children's story is believed to be the origin. The expression was in common usage by the early 1900s.

Grinning like a Cheshire Cat

MEANING: to be very pleased with oneself and smile broadly without any inhibition

IN CONTEXT: Joel was so happy after winning the award that he couldn't stop *grinning like a Cheshire cat.*

Grinning like a Cheshire cat has mixed origins. There is no such breed of feline, but the expression began because all cheeses produced in Cheshire, England, since the 12th century had the face of a grinning cat stamped on them (this is also thought to be the origin of the phrase "cheesy grin"). "Grinning like a Cheshire cat" was first expressed in words by Peter Pindar in his 1795 work *A Pair of Lyric Epistles*, but it wasn't until 1865 that the saying reached worldwide popularity. That was in Lewis Carroll's *Alice's Adventures in Wonderland*, where the mysterious Cheshire Cat appears and disappears, gradually fading away until only its enormous grin remains.

Curry Favor

MEANING: doing acts to attempt to gain favor or support

IN CONTEXT: An election was looming so the government lowered taxes in an attempt to *curry favor* with the voters.

Having nothing to do with Indian food, **curry favor** has its origins in the 1310 French poem by Gervais du Bus entitled "Le Roman de Fauvel" (which translates to "The Romance of Fauvel"). When someone grooms and dresses a horse it is known as "currying." In the poem, Fauvel was the name of a vain and ambitious half-man, half-horse who deceives the leaders of the state. In order to bow to Fauvel and keep on his good side, the people would stroke and groom his coat— they were "currying Fauvel." Eventually, this became currying favor.

Ignorance Is Bliss

MEANING: what you don't know won't hurt you

IN CONTEXT: I never knew eating too much salt was bad for you. *Ignorance is bliss*, I suppose.

Ignorance is bliss derives from the world of poetry. Thomas Gray was an 18th century English poet and professor at Cambridge University. In his 1742 poem "Ode on a Distant Prospect of Eton College" he wrote, "Thought would destroy their paradise. No more where ignorance is bliss, tis folly to be wise." It was that poem that brought about the expression that is so common today.

Go See a Man about a Dog

MEANING: to leave for some unmentioned purpose, usually to go to the toilet

IN CONTEXT: Uncle Pete didn't want Tim to know where he was going, so he told Tim that he was *going to see a man about a dog*.

Go see a man about a dog has its origins in the theater. *Flying Scud* was a popular 1866 production by successful Irish playwright Dion Boucicault. On a number of occasions during the play, whenever the lead character found  himself in an awkward situation that he wanted to get out of, he would say "I've got to go see a man about a dog." This was met with much amusement by audiences. The play was shown in both London and New York, and people soon copied the expression to comic effect when they didn't want to disclose their whereabouts.

Goody-Two-Shoes

MEANING: someone who is virtuous in a smug manner

IN CONTEXT: Jane never did anything wrong at school and she always smiled when we got into trouble. She was such a *goody-two-shoes*.

Goody-two-shoes derives from the 1765 children's book *The History of Little Goody-Two-Shoes*, written by Oliver Goldsmith. It tells the story of Margery Meanwell, an orphan who can only afford one shoe. She is given a pair of shoes by a rich man, and in her excitement, delightedly exclaims "Two shoes, two shoes!" She repeats this to everyone she meets, earning her the nickname "Goody-Two-Shoes." She eventually finds fortune by marrying a wealthy widower. The expression came to mean anyone who was piously virtuous by the early 20th century.

CHAPTER 10
Bring Home the Bacon: Culinary Delights

Best Thing since Sliced Bread

MEANING: an excellent new idea or invention

IN CONTEXT: This new computer software is the *best thing since sliced bread.*

Best thing since sliced bread began, perhaps unsurprisingly, with the bread business. Otto Frederick Rohwedder of Iowa invented the first bread-slicing machine in 1928. The first commercial use of that machine was by the Chillicothe Baking Company in Missouri. Their product was called Kleen Maid Sliced Bread and was advertised in a local newspaper as "the greatest forward step in the baking industry since bread was wrapped." The bread was an instant success and other bakeries started using the machine, advertising it heavily. Sliced bread became a talking point throughout the country and it is thought that the original marketing slogan soon developed into the popular expression that is used today.

Take the Piss

MEANING: to make a joke about someone or to make someone look stupid

IN CONTEXT: They're always *taking the piss* out of him because he's an ABBA fan.

Take the piss is an expression with bizarre origins. In ancient Siberia, the shamans used a hallucinogenic mushroom in their spiritual ceremonies. Called the *Amanita muscaria*, the sacred mushroom was extremely potent and the human body was unable to withstand its toxins. To get around this obstacle, the shamans would feed large quantities of the mushroom to their reindeer, then wait for the animals to urinate in the snow. The shamans would then eat the urine-soaked snow and become high and nonsensical, without any toxic effects.

Put through the Mill

MEANING: a hardship or rough treatment

IN CONTEXT: He worked eighty hours in the first week of his new job. They really *put him through the mill*.

Put through the mill derives from the flour-making process in medieval England. Before electricity was invented, classical mills were usually powered by water, which turned a large wheel. This turned two heavy circular stones, which were laid on top of each other. Cereal seeds were fed through the top stone and they would be ground finely to produce flour. By the 1800s, being put through the mill came to refer to a person undergoing a hardship, similar to the process of being ground down like a grain in a mill.

Broach a Subject

MEANING: to raise a topic with someone, often in awkward circumstances

IN CONTEXT: I hate to be the one to *broach this* with you, but you have lettuce in your teeth.

To **broach a subject** began in the alehouses of London. The word "broach" derives from the Old French word *broche*, meaning "a pointed weapon or implement." In order to draw beer from a barrel, a publican would hammer a wooden peg into the bottom of the barrel, which allowed a tap to be inserted from which the beer could then start to flow. This wooden peg was called a broach and the technique was known as "broaching the barrel." Later, this phrase evolved to refer to the opening up of any new subject of conversation.

Take the Cake

MEANING: to achieve something; to do something outrageous

IN CONTEXT: I worked hard all day then my boss questioned what I'd been doing. That really *takes the cake*.

Sometimes said ironically, **take the cake** originated with the days of slavery in America during the 19th century. At parties held by wealthy white landowners, it was a tradition for married slaves to walk in a procession around a cake in a form of competition. The slaves would be judged, and the couple who was considered the most graceful would get to take the cake as a prize. This is also the origin of the expressions *cake walk* and *piece of cake*, both of which mean "something easily accomplished," as while these tasks were demeaning, the competition required very little effort.

Hair of the Dog

MEANING: an alcoholic drink intended to cure a hangover

IN CONTEXT: Phil felt so bad the day after the party that his only hope was to have a *hair of the dog*.

Hair of the dog is a contraction of the full expression "the hair of the dog that bit you." Its origin lies in medieval English medicine. It was believed that if someone was bitten by a rabid dog, any ill effects would be cured by rubbing the same dog's hair into the infected wound, which would then heal. Despite the obvious risk of being bitten again while acquiring the hair, this practice persisted for years. Eventually it came to be used in relation to people having a couple of drinks to cure a hangover, a remedy that often has temporary success.

Doesn't Cut the Mustard

MEANING: to not perform up to expectations or the required standard

IN CONTEXT: We need a better pitcher. This one just *doesn't cut the mustard*.

Doesn't cut the mustard is an expression with many potential origins. Some say it is a corruption of the military phrase "pass muster," meaning "pass an inspection," but the likely beginnings actually involve the mustard plant. The mustard plant grows very close to the ground and has a particularly tough and stringy stem. They grow densely together and are one of the hardest plants to reap. Before the advent of machinery, farmers would have to bend low all day or even work on their knees to harvest the plant. Once a worker became too old and weak to carry out the arduous task, it was said that he doesn't cut the mustard. The phrase was being used figuratively in America by the end of the 19th century.

Piping Hot

MEANING: extremely hot, usually referring to food

IN CONTEXT: Don't touch the pie yet. It's just come out of the oven and is *piping hot*.

Some believe that **piping hot** owes its beginnings to ceremonial meals in Scotland, where dishes are often brought to the table while bagpipes are playing—they are "piped in." However, this is not the origin. It actually derives from the whistling or sizzling noise made by steam as it escapes from very hot food or the spout of a boiling kettle. This sound is similar to that of high-pitched pipe organs in large churches. The first written recording of the expression was by the English writer Geoffrey Chaucer in his 1386 work *Canterbury Tales*, which referred to "wafers piping hot out of the gleed," the gleed being the fire.

Go Cold Turkey

MEANING: to quit something abruptly

IN CONTEXT: David found it difficult to stop drinking gradually, so he decided to *go cold turkey*.

Go cold turkey began with the symptoms that people exhibit during drug withdrawal. When someone suddenly stops taking drugs after a prolonged use, the addict's blood flows to the internal organs as a survival tactic. This leaves the skin hard and pale with goosebumps all over, so it resembles a plucked, cold turkey. The phrase was used in the medical sense from as early as the 1920s and became a figurative expression about quitting anything—from drugs, to alcohol, to chocolate—by the 1950s.

Propose a Toast

MEANING: a ritual in which a drink is taken in someone's honor

IN CONTEXT: The father of the bride *proposed a toast* to the new couple.

Propose a toast began in the 12th century. The quality of wine at the time was not high and varied considerably. In order to soak up some of the acidity and improve the flavor, a piece of spiced toast was placed in a wine jug, or small pieces were placed in wine glasses. By the 17th century in England, the practice of proposing a toast to someone emerged. The glass would be raised, as it is today, and it was usually a lady who was toasted. The idea was that she became a figurative piece of toast that flavored the wine.

Gone to Pot

MEANING: become ruined; no longer of any use

IN CONTEXT: This beer is five years old and it can't be drunk. It's all *gone to pot*.

Gone to pot originated in the 16th century and has culinary beginnings. Before refrigeration existed, meat did not last as long as it does today, and after a couple of days would harden and become inedible. Such meat that was on the verge of spoiling would be chopped up into small pieces and cooked in a pot to make stew. Meat that was used in this way was referred to as having gone to pot. The first recorded usage of the expression was by William Tyndale, the English scholar. In his 1530 work *An Answer Unto Sir Thomas More's Dialogue*, he wrote, "Then goeth a part of ye little flocke to pot, and the rest scatter."

Don't Teach Your Grandmother to Suck Eggs

MEANING: don't offer advice to a more experienced person

IN CONTEXT: I've been fixing cars since before you were born. *Don't teach your grandmother to suck eggs.*

Don't teach your grandmother to suck eggs began hundreds of years ago before advanced dentistry techniques were common. In those days, dental hygiene was not very good and dentures were expensive. When a poor person got old and their teeth fell out, they were left with only gums. One of the easiest foods to eat without teeth was a hard-boiled egg that the person could suck down. It was often grandparents who were seen doing this and, through years of practice, they became experts at eating eggs this way. The phrase was first recorded in John Stevens' 1707 translation of the collected comedies of the Spanish playwright Francisco de Quevedo, which contained the line, "You would have me teach my Grandame to suck Eggs."

Bring Home the Bacon

MEANING: to earn money for one's family; to be successful

IN CONTEXT: I had been at my job for ten years, but after my promotion I finally started *bringing home the bacon.*

Bring home the bacon began in the village of Dunmow in Essex, England, in the year 1104. In that year, a noblewoman named Juga offered a side of

bacon, known as a flitch, to any married couple in England who could honestly say that they had lived in complete marital harmony without a cross word being spoken for the preceding year and one day. The tradition became known as the Dunmow Flitch Trials. The Trials are still held every four years, the candidates having to prove their worth before a jury of twelve. If successful, they bring home the bacon. In over 500 years, there have only been eight winners.

Eat Humble Pie

MEANING: to act submissively in admitting an error, often in humiliation

IN CONTEXT: I had been so adamant, but when I was proven to be wrong I had to *eat humble pie* and admit my mistake.

To **eat humble pie** has rather distasteful culinary origins. In medieval feasts, there was a definite hierarchy with the food. The lord of the manor and his guests from the upper echelon of society were served the finest cuts of meat, usually venison. Known at the time as "umbles," the reviled offal and entrails would be baked in a pie. Diners who were out of favor or thought to be of a lower class would be served the umble pie. They were often humiliated when their plate arrived and they realized what they were eating. While mentions of umble pie were made by Samuel Pepys in the 17th century and Charles Dickins in the 19th century, it eventually became humble pie, probably because it sounded similar and was related to the feelings involved.

Give a Cold Shoulder

MEANING: an unfriendly reception; a display of indifference

IN CONTEXT: Pamela was late to the party yet again, so we all *gave her the cold shoulder.*

Give a cold shoulder has its origins in the medieval banquets held by noblemen in England. It was not uncommon for the aristocracy to hold feasts for hundreds of people. The feasts often lasted a number of days, and the host would provide an array of choice hot meats for his guests. In order to signal the end of the gathering, the host would direct the kitchen to serve slices of cold shoulder mutton to the people. This was a customary way of informing everyone that the party was over, rather than doing the uncivilized thing of going around the gathering and telling them all in person. While in modern times giving a cold shoulder is considered rude, back then it was actually a polite gesture.

Mind Your P's and Q's

MEANING: be on your best behavior

IN CONTEXT: Simon was meeting his in-laws for the first time so he knew he had better *mind his p's and q's.*

Mind your p's and q's is an expression with many possible origins that are often disputed. The most compelling of these is its association with drinking. It stems from the English taverns of the 17th century when publicans would chalk up what people were drinking, either a pint or a quart, on a tally slate. At the end of the night, the patron would pay for the number and type of drinks on the slate. Because a quart was a larger and more costly measure than a pint, patrons would advise the bartender to mind their p's and q's to ensure the correct drinks had been chalked up so they weren't being overcharged.

Flavor of the Month

MEANING: something in fashion for a fleeting time; the latest thing

IN CONTEXT: She was the *flavor of the month* at her new school until Gloria enrolled.

Often said in a mockingly disdainful way, **flavor of the month** began in the 1930s with American advertising campaigns for ice-cream companies. To encourage customers into their parlors, ice-cream companies ran slogans promoting reduced prices on certain flavors that were less popular. The price of a particular flavor would be dropped for a month-long period in an attempt to increase sales. The price-reduced ice cream would be promoted as the flavor of the month. So successful was this method in increasing sales that by the 1950s, every major American ice-cream company was using the slogan.

CHAPTER 11
Apple of Your Eye:
Biblical Times

The Eleventh Hour

MEANING: the latest possible time; the last minute

IN CONTEXT: I handed in my report at *the eleventh hour* and just made the deadline.

The eleventh hour is an expression with biblical origins. It is from the parable of the laborers in Matthew 20:1-16. The reference reads "And about the eleventh hour he went out, and found others standing idle, and saith unto them, Why stand ye here all the day idle?" At that time, the working day for manual laborers was twelve hours. In a last-ditch attempt to finish the day's scheduled work on time, workers were sometimes hired at the eleventh hour of the day and, because of the urgency, they were paid the same amount as if they had worked the full day.

Wolf in Sheep's Clothing

MEANING: someone who hides a malicious intent while pretending to be friendly and peaceful

IN CONTEXT: Rob appeared to have good intentions, but Beatrice suspected he might be a *wolf in sheep's clothing*.

Wolf in sheep's clothing is an expression from the Bible. It is from Matthew 7:15 and part of the Sermon on the Mount when Jesus says, "Beware of false prophets, which come to you in sheep's clothing, but inwardly they are ravening wolves." The phrase is well-known from one of Aesop's fables, in which a wolf covered in the skin of a sheep is able to deceive the shepherd and sneak into the flock. Once in, the wolf immediately eats a lamb.

Doubting Thomas

MEANING: someone who will not believe anything without strong proof

IN CONTEXT: The house sale was agreed, but Sean was such a *doubting Thomas* that he wouldn't accept it until the money changed hands.

The expression **doubting Thomas** stems from John 20:27 in the Bible. Saint Thomas was one of the Twelve Apostles of Christ, but he would not believe the resurrection of Jesus until he had firsthand physical evidence. This was despite Jesus appearing and speaking. In order to verify the resurrection, Jesus let Thomas touch the wound that a Roman soldier had made while Jesus was on the cross. "Be not faithless, but believing," Jesus said to him. It was only then that Thomas became a believer.

Baptism of Fire

MEANING: an intense introduction to something

IN CONTEXT: His first swimming final was against the world champion in front of 40,000 people. It was a real *baptism of fire*.

Baptism of fire is an expression that relates to the 16th-century Protestant Christian martyrs. They were burned at the stake by Catholics who believed that the practice gave the martyrs a form of baptism before they were judged by

God. Napoleon was the first to use the expression, although he spoke of le baptême du fer, a "baptism of iron." The phrase is often now applied to military situations and a soldier's first experience of war.

Fly in the Ointment

MEANING: a small defect or drawback that spoils something larger

IN CONTEXT: We had spent weeks preparing for the road trip, but at the time of departure there was a slight *fly in the ointment*: there was no gas in the car.

To have a **fly in the ointment** is an expression that originates from the Bible. Ecclesiastes 10:1 includes the phrase, "Dead flies cause the ointment of the apothecary to send forth a stinking savor." Apothecaries were the forerunners to modern-day chemists, and they dispensed various ointments that were used as medical remedies. These ointments were usually prepared in large vats. Generally being very particular about hygiene, the apothecaries believed that a single fly found floating in the ointment would ruin the entire batch.

The Writing Is on the Wall

MEANING: a bad outcome is likely

IN CONTEXT: Neil thought he'd gotten away with the robbery, but when the police knocked on his door, he knew *the writing was on the wall*.

The writing is on the wall is a biblical expression from Chapter 5 of the Book of Daniel. According to Babylonian legend, during a bout of drunken revelry, King Belshazzar drank wine from a sacred vessel that had been taken from the Temple in Jerusalem. As he did this, a mysterious disembodied hand appeared and wrote four words on the palace wall: "mene mene tekel upharsin." Unable to fathom the meaning of the words, the King called for the Hebrew prophet, Daniel. Daniel told Belshazzar that the King had blasphemed God by drinking from the sacred vessel and so God had sent the hand. He then explained the message to the King: God had numbered Belshazzar's days and his kingdom would be lost. Shortly afterward, the King was defeated and slain, and the parable became known as the story of the writing on the wall.

A Little Bird Told Me

MEANING: an implied secret or private source of knowledge

IN CONTEXT: *A little bird told me* that Jake is planning on leaving the company soon.

A little bird told me is originally a reference from the Bible. While the words do not appear verbatim, Ecclesiastes 10:20 includes this line: "for a bird of the air shall carry the voice, and that which hath wings shall tell the matter." There is also a story from the Book of Kings in the Bible that involves a messenger bird. King Solomon summoned every bird to appear before him. They all did, except for the lapwing, who later explained that he had been with the Queen of Sheba, who was making plans to visit the King. Excited by this, Solomon made preparations to receive the

Queen, and this information was passed back to the Queen by the lapwing. Facilitated by the little bird, the King and the Queen finally met. The expression was then used in literature from the 16th century.

Take under Your Wing

MEANING: to nurture, help, or guide someone

IN CONTEXT: When I was new to the company, Geoff *took me under his wing* and showed me the ropes.

Take under your wing is an expression that has origins in the Bible, taken from the nurturing practice of mother birds who shelter chicks beneath their wings. The phrase derives from Matthew 23:37 and Jesus's wish to protect the people of Jerusalem. In that passage Jesus says, "Oh Jerusalem, Jerusalem, you that kill the prophets and stone them which are sent to you. How often I have wanted to gather your children together as a hen protects her chicks beneath her wings, but you wouldn't let me."

Stumbling Block

MEANING: an obstacle or hindrance

IN CONTEXT: The yacht was perfect for us, but the exorbitant price was too big a *stumbling block*.

Stumbling block is another expression that stems from the Bible. The popular phrase is referred to in two instances. Romans 14:13 says, "Therefore let us stop passing judgment on one another. Instead, make up your mind not to put any stumbling block or obstacle in the way of a brother or sister."

Leviticus 19:14 also contains a reference: "You shall not curse the deaf nor place a stumbling block before the blind; you shall fear your God—I am your Lord." The expression was being used figuratively from the early 1500s.

By the Skin of Your Teeth

MEANING: by the narrowest of margins

IN CONTEXT: My car skidded across the road in the wet conditions and I missed the lamppost *by the skin of my teeth.*

Most often used in relation to an escape from disaster, **by the skin of your teeth** is a biblical expression from Job 19:20. Satan makes a bet with God claiming that he can get Job to curse God's name. God accepts and Satan does his worst in torturing Job, covering him in excruciating boils. Writhing in pain, at one point Job cries, "I am nothing but skin and bone. I have escaped with only the skin of my teeth." It is thought the likely reference is to Job's gums, the skin that held his teeth in place, and obviously a very narrow margin.

Play the Fool

MEANING: to act in a silly way, usually to amuse others

IN CONTEXT: The teacher told Jed to sit down and stop *playing the fool.*

Play the fool rose from the Bible and the book of Samuel 26:12. It tells the story of King Saul, who follows David with the intention of killing him. Admitting this, Saul says, "I have sinned. Return, my son David, for I will not harm you again because my life is precious in your eyes this day. Behold, I have played the fool and have committed a serious error." Playing the fool in this original instance involved sinister intentions, but later evolved to simply mean tomfoolery.

Devil's Advocate

MEANING: someone who argues against a point for the sake of it

IN CONTEXT: Ben is a really annoying person to have a discussion with as he's always playing the *devil's advocate*.

Devil's advocate has its origins with the Roman Catholic Church. Since 1587 there has been a prescribed procedure for every candidate seeking sainthood. Before the Church determined whether to grant the sainthood, two representatives were appointed to argue the case. Arguing in favor of the proposed canonization was the advocatus dei, or God's advocate, and presenting every possible argument against it was the advocatus diaboli, or devil's advocate. Usage of the expression in the wider sense began by the mid-18th century.

Makes Your Hair Stand on End

MEANING: something frightening

IN CONTEXT: Whenever I see sharks on TV, they *make my hair stand on end*.

Having your hair stand on end is a physiological phenomenon that occurs as a reaction to the cold, excitement, or fear. Known colloquially as goosebumps (although the technical term is horripilation), the skin contracts and makes a person's hairs stand upright. The expression itself has biblical origins and derives from Job 4:15 in the Old Testament: "A spirit glided past my face, and the hair on my body stood on end." The phrase became widespread in 1603 with Shakespeare's play *Hamlet*. In it he referred to a harrowing tale which would make "each particular hair to stand on end, like the quills upon the fretful porcupine."

Bless You

MEANING: said to someone who sneezes

IN CONTEXT: I sneezed on the bus and the lady next to me said "*bless you*."

Often said as "God bless you," **bless you** has religious origins. In medieval times it was believed that a sneeze would thrust a person's soul from the body. God bless you was said to protect the unguarded soul from the devil until the person's body regained it. Another school of thought at the time was that a sneeze was the expulsion of an evil spirit from the body. The person was blessed in the hope that the evil spirit would be unable to return to the blessed body. The expression became widespread during the Great Plague of London in 1665. Sneezing was thought to be a symptom of the Black Death, so "God bless you" was said to try to ward off the disease.

Drop in the Ocean

MEANING: a very small proportion of the whole

IN CONTEXT: The media room was expensive, but it was a *drop in the ocean* compared to the cost of the whole house.

Originally said as a "drop in the bucket," **drop in the ocean** is a biblical expression. Isaiah 40:15 says "Behold, the nations are like a drop from a bucket, and are regarded as a speck of dust on the scales; Behold, He lifts up the islands like fine dust." The phrase became a drop in the ocean by the early 1800s. The amended phrase was then popularized by Charles Dickens in his 1843 book *A Christmas Carol* when he wrote, "The dealings of my trade were but a drop of water in the comprehensive ocean of my business!"

Apple of Your Eye

MEANING: someone who is cherished above all else

IN CONTEXT: Her grandson is the *apple of her eye*.

Apple of your eye is an expression that dates back centuries. In Old English, the pupil of the eye was known as the apple. This was perhaps because it is round, much like an apple. Sight was regarded as the most essential of the senses, and so the apple was cherished and protected. Any damage to it was considered abhorrent. In the figurative sense, it was referred to by King Alfred the Great of Wessex in AD 885, and it was used by Shakespeare in *A Midsummer Night's Dream* in 1605. But its first reference is from the

Bible in Deuteronomy 32:10, which reads, "he led him about, he instructed him, he kept him as the apple of his eye."

Wash Your Hands of It

MEANING: to end all involvement with something

IN CONTEXT: The project had dragged on for six years and Kerry couldn't wait to *wash her hands of it*.

While the expression is not directly stated, **wash your hands of it** derives from Matthew 27:24 in the Bible. In the trial of Jesus, Pontius Pilate was in charge of sentencing. But he refused to condemn Jesus and declared to the crowd that Jesus was innocent. Pilate saw that his pleas were being ignored and an uproar was starting. The people demanded an execution, and, not wanting to be a part of it, Pilate takes a bowl of water and washes his hands, announcing, "I am innocent of this man's blood. It is your responsibility."

Straight and Narrow

MEANING: proper conduct and moral integrity

IN CONTEXT: Ever since getting out of jail, Carl had been on the *straight and narrow*.

Straight and narrow is a phrase that comes from the Bible. It was formally "strait and narrow," with strait meaning "narrow or confining," as in a straitjacket. Matthew 7:14 reads, "Broad is the way that is the path of destruction but strait is the gate, and narrow is the way, which leadeth to the house of God." It describes the way and the gate to Heaven as being narrow, meaning that one must tread carefully in order to make it there and enter.

Enter the Lions' Den

MEANING: a hostile or dangerous place or situation, particularly because of the people there

IN CONTEXT: My work interview was with three of the top professionals in the city. I felt like I was walking *into the lions' den*.

Enter the lions' den originates from the story of Daniel in the Lions' Den, from Daniel 6:16 in the Old Testament. In the story, Daniel is betrayed and sentenced to death for publicly praying to his own God. While he was a friend of Daniel's, the King has no choice but to condemn Daniel to death. "So the King gave the order, and they brought Daniel and threw him into the lions' den. The King said to Daniel, "May your God, whom you serve continually, rescue you!" At daybreak, the King hurried back to see if God had saved his friend. Daniel remained unscathed, and said that God had sent an angel to close the jaws of the lions. The King then cast those who conspired against Daniel into the lions' den.

The Powers that Be

MEANING: the people who are in authority

IN CONTEXT: I have put my application in and am just waiting for *the powers that be* to make a decision.

The powers that be is another phrase that derives from the Bible. Romans 13:1 says, "Let every soul submit himself unto the authority of the higher powers. For there is no power but of God. The powers that be are ordained of God. Whosoever therefore resists power, resists the ordinance of God."

Kiss of Death

MEANING: an action that will lead to certain failure

IN CONTEXT: When the major banks all hinted that they might raise interest rates, it was like a *kiss of death* to the stock market.

Kiss of death began with the Bible and the betrayal of Jesus by Judas. In Matthew 26:47-49, Judas Iscariot kisses Jesus on the cheek as a way of identifying him to the Roman soldiers. As a result of that kiss, Jesus was arrested and crucified. This practice found its way to the Mafia bosses of Sicily. A kiss from the Don meant the person would soon be killed. Originally known as a "Judas kiss," the expression was changed in the 1940s.

In Seventh Heaven

MEANING: pure happiness; truly delighted

IN CONTEXT: It had been a long flight to Mexico, but as I lazed on the beach with a cold drink I was truly *in seventh heaven.*

In seventh heaven owes its origins to the religions of Islam and Judaism. According to Muslim beliefs, there are seven heavens, each depicted as being made of a different material with prophets resident in each. The first heaven is made of silver and is the home of Adam and Eve. The second heaven is made of gold, and in it resides John the Baptist and Jesus. The heavens keep rising, with the sixth being the home of Moses. The seventh heaven is the most glorious of all and is occupied by Abraham, who presides over everything. Jewish mysticism also embraces the concept of seven heavens, with the seventh being the most exalted and the home of God and his holy angels, a place of complete and eternal bliss.

Blind Leading the Blind

MEANING: incompetent people advising or guiding others who are equally incapable

IN CONTEXT: Gary was never any good at tennis, but now he's coaching his young son. That's a case of the *blind leading the blind*.

Blind leading the blind is an expression from the Bible, but it may have an earlier source. One of Jesus's teachings from Matthew 15:14 reads, "Let them alone: They be blind leaders of blind. And if the blind lead the blind, both shall fall into the ditch." It is thought that the Bible took the phrase from the Upanishads, which were sacred Hindu treatises written as far back as 800 BC. The ancient text of *Katha Upanishad* includes this line: "Abiding in the midst of ignorance, thinking themselves wise and learned, fools go aimlessly hither and thither, like blind led by the blind."

CHAPTER 12
Caught Red-Handed: Law and Order

Short Shrift

MEANING: to give little consideration to

IN CONTEXT: He took a whole week to apologize, so when he did I gave him *short shrift* and didn't even respond.

Often mistakenly said as "shift," **short shrift** dates from the criminal world of the 17th century. A "shrift" is a confession given to a priest in order to obtain absolution. It comes from the verb shrive, the past tense of which is shrove—Shrove Tuesday is when people go to confession. In the 17th century, as soon as criminals were convicted and sentenced, they were sent to the gallows to be hanged. There was usually a priest waiting with the executioner and the prisoners were allowed a very short time to confess their sins in the last minutes of their life. They were given a short shrift before they were killed.

To Double Cross

MEANING: a deliberate betrayal, usually by a previous partner; a violation of a promise

IN CONTEXT: The two thieves planned to split the money, but one *double crossed* the other and fled with it all.

There is some conjecture as to the true origins of the expression **to double cross**. Some say it began with racehorse jockeys who would receive money to lose a race, but then go on to win. They would cross themselves twice as they passed the winning post, as a plea to God to forgive them for their double deception. However, the likely beginnings are from the 18th-century London bounty hunter Jonathan Wild. Wild had a monopoly on crime at the time, famed for operating on both sides of the law. Known as the "Thief-Taker General," Wild kept meticulous records of all the criminals he did business with, paying for information that advanced his extensive network. If any criminal on the list displeased Wild in any way, he would place a cross next to his name in the book of thieves. A second cross meant that the criminal had outlived his usefulness, and Wild would turn him into the authorities and claim the reward. Wild himself was eventually betrayed and was hanged in 1725. The first written reference to double cross as an expression was by David Garrick in his 1768 play *The Irish Widow*.

Hung, Drawn, and Quartered

MEANING: a form of torture ending in death

IN CONTEXT: I'll be *hung, drawn, and quartered* if I don't submit my work on time again.

Hung, drawn, and quartered (technically hanged, drawn, and quartered) was a form of punishment and execution in England from the 13th century until 1870. It was reserved for anyone convicted of treason, and the executions were a popular public spectacle. The process involved hanging the man until he was almost dead, before disemboweling him (known as "drawing'"), then chopping off his head and cutting his torso into four parts. The remains were often displayed in prominent places across the country as a warning to others. Many famous men were victims of this draconian punishment, including the famous traitor, Guy

Fawkes, and the Scottish patriot, William Wallace. The expression developed into its present-day figurative use by the 17th century.

By Hook or By Crook

MEANING: by whatever means necessary, fair or unfair

IN CONTEXT: I'm going to get to the train station on time, *by hook or by crook*.

By hook or by crook originates from medieval England. Hooks and crooks were long-handled tools used by lower class people in the fields. A hook was a blunt device used by a reaper for holding or pulling, and a crook had a bent end and was used by shepherds to tend to sheep. It was law at the time that no trees or branches were allowed to be cut from the royal forests for firewood. However, peasants were allowed to take whatever deadwood they could gather with either a reaper's billhook or a shepherd's crook—anything by hook or by crook was permissible.

To Be Screwed

MEANING: to be cheated

IN CONTEXT: That car is only worth $10,000. You really *got screwed* on that deal.

To be screwed derives from a 19th-century form of punishment. At the time, English prisons were notoriously tough, with "hard labor" meaning just that. A common practice to punish inmates was to have them turn a crank handle for hours at a time. This was hard enough work as it was, but it could be made even more difficult by a guard tightening a screw, which increased the resistance of the crank. Any prisoner who was particularly bad or disliked by the prison staff would usually be screwed. This is also the origin of the phrase *to tighten the screw*.

Take for a Ride

MEANING: to cheat or deceive someone

IN CONTEXT: I trusted my accountant to invest the money for me, but he *took me for a ride* and I lost the lot.

Take for a ride originated during the era of Prohibition in America. During the 1920s, criminality was high, with gangs dealing in bootlegging and other illegal activities. Competition for market share was strong and gang warfare was rife. Any rival gang member who displeased another chieftain would commonly be invited by a henchman to go for a ride. The idea was that the men would drive in a car to a secluded place, where they could talk matters over and resolve any differences. But this was usually just a cover, and the victim rarely returned.

Laughing Stock

MEANING: an object of ridicule and humiliation

IN CONTEXT: Her constant mistakes at work had made her the *laughing stock* of the company.

Laughing stock originated from a medieval form of punishment in England. Most villages had stocks set up in the public square. The stocks comprised two sliding boards with holes in them that were secured on a wooden frame. The hands and feet of the victim were placed in the holes, rendering him unable to escape or move freely. Petty criminals were put in the stocks so the town people could gather around, laughing and humiliating the person, even throwing rotten vegetables at them. The phrase laughing stock had developed into its current use by the early 1500s. In Sir Philip Sidney's 1533 critique *An Apology for Poetry*, he wrote "Poetry is fallen to be the laughing stock of children."

Pull the Wool over Your Eyes

MEANING: to trick or deceive

IN CONTEXT: My lawyer said he'd charge a flat fee, but he *pulled the wool over my eyes* and ended up charging me for a lot of extras.

Pull the wool over your eyes relates to the elaborate wigs that people wore in the 17th century. The wigs had a thick, woolly appearance. The social standing of a man was sometimes judged by the size of his wig—the bigger it was, the more wealth the man was thought to have.

By wearing large wigs, men were advertising their wealth and became a target for petty criminals. A large wig could also be pulled down more easily. A tactic employed by some criminals was to creep up behind a man and pull the wig down over his eyes. This would temporarily render the victim unable to see, making him easier to rob.

There but for the Grace of God Go I

MEANING: the acknowledgment of somebody else's misfortune and suggesting that it could have easily happen to you as well

IN CONTEXT: So many people went bankrupt during the financial crisis that I couldn't help but think that *there but for the grace of God go I.*

The expression **there but for the grace of God go I** is credited to the Protestant preacher and martyr, John Bradford. Queen Mary I's restoration of the Catholic Church in England saw the persecution of many Protestants. Bradford was one of them, and he was imprisoned in the Tower of London on spurious charges. Each time he saw other prisoners being led off to be executed, he was heard to utter, "There but for the grace of God goes John Bradford." However, Bradford did not enjoy God's grace for long, because he was burned at the stake at Smithfield market in London on July 1, 1555. Sir Arthur Conan Doyle used the phrase in his 1891 Sherlock Holmes story "The Boscombe Valley Mystery," which led to its common usage.

Read the Riot Act

MEANING: to berate harshly

IN CONTEXT: It was the third time in a week that Lee had been late for work so I really *read the riot act* to him.

In the 18th century, **reading the riot act** would literally happen. Instituted in 1715, the Riot Act gave British magistrates the authority to label any group of more than twelve people a threat to the peace. Formally described as "an act for preventing tumults and riotous assemblies, and for the more speedy and effectual punishing of rioters," a public official would read aloud a section of the Riot Act, which demanded people "immediately disperse themselves, and peaceably to depart to their habitations, or to their lawful business." Anyone who remained after one hour was subject to removal by force and arrest. The punishments for ignoring the Riot Act were severe—penal servitude for not less than three years, or imprisonment with hard labor for up to two years. The law was put to the test during the infamous Peterloo Massacre in 1819, when a cavalry unit attacked protesters who ignored the reading. But like many other times over history, at the trial the rioters claimed not to have heard the reading because of the loud raucous. The Riot Act remained in effect until 1973.

Pay through the Nose

MEANING: pay an excessive amount for something

IN CONTEXT: It was peak season at the hotel so we *paid through the nose* for our room.

Pay through the nose dates all the way back to the 9th century when the Vikings invaded Ireland. The Danish had extraordinarily harsh tax laws, which they imposed on any land they invaded. With the invasion of Ireland, they applied a particularly high tax known as the "Nose Tax." The punishment for evading the Nose Tax was draconian and perverse. Anyone refusing to pay the tax had their nose slit from tip to eyebrow. The people had a choice: either pay the tax, or pay through the nose.

Paint the Town Red

MEANING: to go out and celebrate or get drunk

IN CONTEXT: Ed finished his exams today so he's gone out to *paint the town red*.

Paint the town red owes its origin to a legendary night of revelry. In 1837, the Marquess of Waterford, known as the "Mad Marquess" because of his erratic behavior, went out with his friends in the English town of Melton Mowbray. The group went berserk on a vandalism spree around the town. They broke windows, pulled off door knockers, and smashed flowerpots. Unsatisfied with that, they acquired some red paint and painted a swan statue, a number of house doors, and even a tollgate. The Marquess later paid compensation for the damage caused, but he had painted the town red and would never live it down.

Rule of Thumb

MEANING: a rough and useful principle based on experience rather scientific calculation

IN CONTEXT: As a *rule of thumb*, new plants should be watered daily for the first two weeks.

Rule of thumb has many potential origins. The practice of using the thumb for measurements has existed for centuries—the Romans are said to have used the length from the thumb's last knuckle to the tip as a measurement for one inch, and before the advent of thermometers, brewmasters would test the temperature of fermenting beer with their thumbs. While the thumb had been used in this way since ancient times, the saying did not get coined until 1782. In that year, Justice Francis Buller of the King's Bench in England delivered a judgment that formalized the age-old maxim of English law that allowed a man to beat his wife provided that he used a stick no thicker than his thumb. Buller was accused of being prejudiced and was later attacked in a satirical cartoon where he was characterized as "Judge Thumb." The expression rule of thumb became widespread from that time on.

Haul Someone Over the Coals

MEANING: to severely reprimand someone for something they've done

IN CONTEXT: He was late for training three days in a row, so the coach really *hauled him over the coals*.

To **haul someone over the coals** originated from the treatment of heretics in the Middle Ages. Heresy is the challenge of the doctrines of an established church, or the practice of unorthodox religions. At that time, heresy was considered a crime against the Church and was punishable by death. However, very few people would admit to it, and the crime was difficult to prove. To combat these evidentiary difficulties, anybody suspected of heresy would be bound and then pulled over a bed of red-hot coals. It was decreed that if the person died, he was obviously a heretic and deserved his fate, but if he survived the torture, God had protected him and he would be set free.

Pipe Dreams

MEANING: an unrealistic hope or plan; a fantasy

IN CONTEXT: I'd always wanted a house in the Bahamas, but deep down I knew it was just a *pipe dream*.

Pipe dreams refers to the dreams experienced by the smokers of opium pipes. Opium is a narcotic drug that produces an analgesic and hypnotic effect. The pipe is the device that the opium is placed in and the vapors are inhaled by smoking the pipe. People under the influence of opium often have vivid and fantastic hallucinations. The expression has been used in America since the late 1800s, when opium smoking was legal. The phrase was first written in a figurative sense in a December 1890 edition of *The Chicago Daily Tribune* referring to man-made flight: "It has been regarded as a pipe dream for a good many years."

Give Someone a Break

MEANING: to give someone a chance or special consideration

IN CONTEXT: I was two marks under the grade but the teacher *gave me a break* and let me pass anyway.

To **give someone a break** derives from medieval street performers. The acts of these men were usually quite energetic and they were given a break halfway through so that they could pass a hat around and collect money from the crowd for their performance. The expression was then taken up by the criminal world in the 1800s. Whenever a felon was about to be released from prison, his friends would collect money together to give to him so he wouldn't be penniless. It was said that he was given a break.

Baker's Dozen

MEANING: thirteen

IN CONTEXT: I like that new bread shop. It always gives you a *baker's dozen.*

Baker's dozen dates all the way back to the 13th century. In 1266 England, King Henry III introduced a law that regulated the price of bread based on  the price of wheat. One of the reasons for this was to stop bakers from selling underweight loaves, something they were reputed to do. The punishment for breach of the law was harsh and could result in the baker being fined, flogged, or put in the stocks. As a safety measure to avoid the draconian penalties, bakers would give an extra loaf of bread for every dozen. The thirteenth loaf was known as the "vantage loaf."

In Cold Blood

MEANING: deliberately and dispassionately; without emotion

IN CONTEXT: The murderer just walked up and shot the man *in cold blood.*

Often used in relation to murder, **in cold blood** dates from the early 18th century. The expression began with the belief that a person's blood heated up when an act of great emotion or passion was committed. This was based on the reddening of the face and the feeling of heat that a person experienced. It was thought that when one could carry out a violent crime without excitement or emotional involvement, the person was acting in cold blood. The phrase was first recorded in Joseph Addison's daily English publication *The Spectator* in 1711, and the word "sangfroid", meaning "cool and calm," comes from the French words for "blood" and "cold."

Red Tape

MEANING: pointless bureaucratic procedures; excessive regulations

IN CONTEXT: I wanted to get a truck license, but with all the *red tape* involved it took months.

Red tape is an expression that has been in existence since the 16th century in Britain. Since that time, legal and official documents have been bound with red ribbon. Documents were rolled in their original condition and sealed with red tape. This was done as a measure to ensure documents had not been tampered with, similar to wax seals in ancient times. Official Vatican documents were also bound in red cloth. To this day, many legal documents are bound with pink- or red-colored material. The phrase was changed into its current form by Charles Dickens, who used it to refer to governmental bureaucracies in a number of his books, including *David Copperfield* in 1849, *Bleak House* in 1853, and *Little Dorrit* in 1857.

Cat and Mouse

MEANING: to toy with; a situation where prey continually escapes its predator but is recaptured

IN CONTEXT: Julie loved to play *cat and mouse* with an admirer, drawing him in and then being indifferent.

Cat and mouse is an expression that began with the British suffragettes who were fighting for the right to vote at the start of the 20th century. Often when a suffragette was imprisoned, she would go on a hunger strike to draw attention to her cause. Embarrassed by this, the government took to force-feeding the prisoners until a better solution was devised. In 1913 the Prisoners (Temporary Discharge for Ill-Health) Act was passed. This allowed the authorities to detain the women until they became ill. The women were then released to recover, but were too weak to protest. By doing this, the government could claim that any harm that resulted from the starvation was entirely the fault of the suffragette. And as soon as the suffragette recovered and began protesting again, she would be sent back to prison. This piece of legislation became known as the "Cat and Mouse Act," and from then on the expression was used.

Kangaroo Court

MEANING: a mock court that disregards due legal process

IN CONTEXT: Instead of being given a fair trial, the foreign drug smuggler was tried in a *kangaroo court*.

Kangaroo court originated with the California Gold Rush of 1849. Crime at the time was common, and there were many illegal gold prospectors who seized the mining claims of others. They were known as "claim jumpers." The gold mines had a lawless atmosphere, but informal courts were set up to dispense a rough and ready form of justice to the claim jumpers. There was a large contingent of Australian prospectors seeking their fortune in California, and this, coupled with the reference to "jumping," gave birth to the naming of the kangaroo court. The term then spread to Britain and was used for any such mock tribunal.

Buying Time

MEANING: to stall; to be evasive in order to gain time

IN CONTEXT: We intentionally prolonged the negotiations to *buy some time* while the exchange rate dropped further.

Buying time originated in England in 1797 when the Duties on Clocks and Watches Act was passed. This act, known as the "Clock Tax," declared that a five-shilling tax would be imposed on every clock or watch in the British Isles. Many clock owners either hid or got rid of their clocks in order to avoid the perverse tax. Sensing an opportunity, tavern owners hung large clocks on their walls, and anyone who wanted to know the time would have to come in. The tavern owners did not mind paying the tax, because people who came in to find out the time were then compelled to purchase a drink. The people would then often stay longer than originally planned, thus they "bought time."

Skeleton in the Closet

MEANING: a shameful secret

IN CONTEXT: Their uncle had once been in jail, which was the family's only *skeleton in the closet*.

Skeleton in the closet has its origins in English medical law. Until the introduction of the Anatomy Act in 1832, it was illegal to dissect a human body for medical research. But in contravention of the law, some doctors did still use corpses for both research and teaching. So as to avoid detection, they were known to store the leftover skeletons in their locked closets. The expression was first used in an article by William Thackeray in *Punch* magazine in 1845 and then in his 1855 book *The Newcomes*, after which the phrase became commonplace.

Have a Beef

MEANING: to have an issue with someone or something

IN CONTEXT: It was twenty years ago at high school that I stole Graham's girlfriend, but he still *has a beef* with me about it.

Have a beef began with the criminal underworld of London in the 18th century. Whenever fellow criminals heard the traditional cry of "stop thief!" in an attempt to help their friend  they would loudly yell "hot beef, hot beef." Known for their cockney rhyming slang, this had the effect of drowning out the original cry and confusing any would-be pursuers, allowing the thief to escape. The term "cry beef" was first defined in the 1811 *Dictionary of the Vulgar Tongue* as "to give the alarm." This was later developed into the expression that we use today.

Put Your Thinking Cap On

MEANING: to think seriously about how to solve a problem; to concentrate

IN CONTEXT: We will all need to *put our thinking caps on* if we're going to find a way out of this situation.

Put your thinking cap on originated with the judges of the early law courts in England. It was customary at the time for a judge to put on a black cap to show the court that he had heard all the evidence in a criminal trial. The cap was a signal that the judge was ready to deliberate his verdict before passing sentence. Because judges were learned men and respected intellectuals, the cap was referred to as a thinking cap. The expression had taken on its broader meaning by the mid-19th century.

Pillar to Post

MEANING: from one place to another

IN CONTEXT: After he joined the army, Joel's family was moved around the country from *pillar to post*.

From **pillar to post** dates back to a brutal form of punishment in medieval England. Each town had a whipping post and a pillory to deal with criminals. Also known as the "stocks," a pillory was a wooden frame with three holes in it. A criminal's head and hands would be placed through the holes and the public would gather around throwing rotten vegetables and eggs at the disgraced man. This may last a number of days. The criminal would then be dragged to the whipping post, where he would receive a public flogging. Originally from "pillory to post," the expression gradually evolved into what we use today.

Caught Red-Handed

MEANING: caught in the act

IN CONTEXT: The criminal was *caught red-handed* coming out of the store with the diamonds in his pocket.

Sometimes said using its Latin equivalent in flagrante delicto, **caught red-handed** derives from 15th-century Scotland. Legislation existed at that time that referred to "red-hand," in relation to offenses where the perpetrator was caught in the act. This stemmed from the evidentiary requirement of needing to find actual blood on the hands of anyone accused of poaching. One Scottish legal commentary from 1674 stated, "If he be not taken red-hand, the sheriff cannot proceed against him." The expression was adapted to being caught red-handed by Sir Walter Scott in his 1819 book *Ivanhoe*, which popularized the saying.

Rings True

MEANING: a story tested and found genuine

IN CONTEXT: Adam said he'd been at the beach, and he did have sand on his feet, so his story *rang true*.

Commonly said as "the ring of truth," **rings true** has its origins with the currency manufacturers of the Middle Ages. At the time, monetary coins were actually made of gold, silver, or other semi-precious metals, with their value depending on the weight of metal they contained. Owing to poor equipment and the scarcity of precious metals, it was difficult to produce coins of a uniform weight and appearance. This provided criminals with an opportunity. They would counterfeit coins by mixing small quantities of gold or silver with a cheaper metal. But when dropped on a stone slab, pure precious metals have a clear sonorous ring, compared with the dull and flat tone of a fake. If someone wanted to test if a coin was genuine, all they had to do was drop it and see if it rang true.

CHAPTER 13

Beat around the Bush: Animals and Nature

Fair Game

MEANING: a legitimate target for attack, ridicule, or pursuit

IN CONTEXT: Anyone who is brave enough to go on that talk show is *fair game*.

Fair game is an expression that began in the 18th century in England. King George III was a keen hunter and introduced a raft of new laws in an attempt to reduce poaching and protect the livestock of upper-class landowners. The King wanted to keep hunting as a privilege of the aristocracy and he made it illegal for anyone, apart from the landowner and his eldest son, to kill

any game animal, such as pheasants or deer. The punishments for any breach of the legislation were severe. Only certain animals were exempt and allowed to be killed by others, like vermin and some birds that were harmful to the landowner's crops. These animals were referred to in the laws as fair game.

Get Your Back Up

MEANING: to get angry or offended

IN CONTEXT: He kept interrupting everything I said and it really *got my back up*.

Get your back up derives from the habits of cats, who arch their backs when they are threatened or angry. This causes their hair to stand on end and makes them appear larger than they actually are. The expression has been used colloquially in Britain since the 18th century and was defined in Francis

Grose's 1788 work *A Classical Dictionary of the Vulgar Tongue* as "His back is up, i.e. he is offended or angry: an expression or idea taken from a cat; that animal, when angry, always raising its back."

Get into a Scrape

MEANING: to be in a difficult or awkward situation through carelessness

IN CONTEXT: I *got into a bit of a scrape* at the grocery store when I went to pay and had no money in my wallet.

Get into a scrape dates back to the early 19th century in England. The countryside at that time was full of wild deer, which were hunted vigorously. To avoid hunters and predators, deer would use their sharp front hooves to scrape and dig out gullies in the ground, in which they would seek cover and be out of sight. These gullies were known as "scrapes" and they were very difficult to see, especially when they became overgrown by foliage. Any hunter either walking or on horseback was liable to fall down into a scrape, which could result in serious injury.

Knock on Wood

MEANING: to express a wish that something will or will not occur

IN CONTEXT: I've not yet lost on the stock market, *knock on wood*.

Sometimes phrased as "touch wood," **knock on wood** is an expression that dates back to the ancient Druids, a race who inhabited England before the Romans. The Druids worshipped trees (in particular, oaks) and held the firm belief that protective spirits lived within trees. Trees, they believed, were sources of good and warded off evil spirits. People in need of good luck would go and touch a tree. Others actually wore small pieces of oak on necklaces so the wood was always in contact with their skin. The expression became commonplace by the 1850s, and Winston Churchill once said that he always liked to be within an arm's length of a piece of wood.

White Elephant

MEANING: an expensive but unwanted possession or thing

IN CONTEXT: My uncle left me a boat in his will, but it turned out to be a *white elephant* as the maintenance costs were huge.

The expression **white elephant** stems from Thailand in the 17th century, when it was known as Siam. Albino elephants were extremely rare and any born in Siam became the property of the King. The elephants were considered sacred and could not be ridden, killed, or put to work. They were also very expensive to feed and house. If the King was displeased with any nobleman, he would gift him a white elephant out of malice. Unable to refuse a royal gift, the nobleman would be forced to care for the useless animal for the rest of his life, which would often lead to financial ruin.

Pecking Order

MEANING: the hierarchy of authority in a group

IN CONTEXT: Kris had only been at the firm a week, but he kept contradicting the senior partners. He clearly didn't know the *pecking order*.

Pecking order is a phrase which began with the farming of chickens. Domestic poultry maintain a strict hierarchy, where the lead hen is able to peck any other for whatever reason without fear of retribution. The other hens are ordered beneath the lead hen and each of them know which hens are lower than them and are thus able to be pecked. This cascades down to the lowest hen, who gets pecked by all the other hens. While this behavior had been observed for centuries, German biologists coined the phrase pecking order in the 1920s and, because of the similarities in human and corporate behavior, the expression had taken on its wider meaning by the 1950s.

Once in a Blue Moon

MEANING: very rarely

IN CONTEXT: Our daughter lives abroad so we only see her *once in a blue moon*.

Once in a blue moon is an expression that is related to the moon, but the color blue has no significance in the origin of the phrase. The moon can appear blue at any time, depending on certain weather conditions, but *The Maine Farmers' Almanac* provides the explanation of the saying. Since 1819, that publication listed the dates of the various moons, for example, the Harvest Moon and the Hunter's Moon.

Typically, there are three full moons for each season—winter, spring, summer, and fall. Because the lunar and the calendar months are not the same, some years had thirteen full moons instead of twelve, and the *Almanac* named (for no apparent reason) the third full moon in the unusual four-moon season as the blue moon. An amateur American astronomer named James Pruett misinterpreted the *Almanac* and described the Blue Moon as the "second full moon in a month" in a 1946 edition of *Sky & Telescope Magazine*. This took hold and is now the accepted definition. A blue moon occurs about every three years.

Swan Song

MEANING: a final accomplishment or performance

IN CONTEXT: Sam is retiring in two months. This rail project will be his *swan song*.

The expression **swan song** derives from the ancient belief that swans spent their entire lives mute and then sang beautifully for the first time just before they died. Both the ancient Greeks and Romans believed this to be the case (Socrates told Plato that the swan's song was an expression of joy), although by AD 77, the Roman philosopher Pliny the Elder wrote in his book *Naturalis Historia* that "observation shows that the story that the dying swan sings is false." Despite this, the poetic imagery of the swan song led many to include it in their works, including Chaucer and Shakespeare. The phrase itself did not come into existence until 1836, when Thomas Carlyle used it in his novel *Sartor Resartus*. It is thought that he based it on *schwanengesang*, the German version of the term.

As Bald as a Badger

MEANING: to have no hair; to be bald

IN CONTEXT: Lou is only thirty, but he's *as bald as a badger* already.

Many believe the expression **as bald as a badger** arose because the top of a badger's head is white, giving the impression of baldness. However, it actually derives from Victorian times, and the original expression was "as bald as a badger's bum." At the time, male face shaving brushes were made with badger's hair, plucked from the badger's rump. Badgers were trapped for this purpose, plucked, and then set free. The hair would grow back, but before it did, it was common in the countryside of England to see bald badgers running about.

To Fly in the Face

MEANING: to go against an accepted belief or practice; to do the opposite of what is expected

IN CONTEXT: Her decision to quit her job and start a new career *flies in the face* of sound judgment.

To fly in the face is a simple expression that has been in use for hundreds of years. It alludes to a defense mechanism used by chickens. When attacked by a fox, a chicken will fly at and around the fox's face. While this seems a paradoxical and dangerous maneuver, it is done in an attempt to distract and confuse the fox.

Make a Beeline for

MEANING: go directly toward something using the fastest route

IN CONTEXT: As soon as Andrew got home from school, he *made a beeline for* the refrigerator.

Make a beeline for originates from the animal kingdom, and as the phrase suggests, the bee. Once a bee discovers a nectar source, it will return to the hive where it performs a peculiar dance to communicate the location to the other bees. After watching this dance, which is a circular pattern that includes the occasional zigzag, the other bees will then make their way directly to the food source in a straight line. Experts believe that bees use the sun to navigate and that the dance performed by the forager bee indicates the angle relative to the sun that the bees should follow, as well as the distance they should go to ensure they fly in a beeline. The expression has been used figuratively since the early 1800s.

Wet behind the Ears

MEANING: to be naïve or inexperienced

IN CONTEXT: Greg is far too young for a job like this. He's still *wet behind the ears*.

Wet behind the ears is a rare example of an expression with very simple origins. The phrase stems from the state of farm animals just after birth. There is a small indentation behind the ears of a newborn horse, calf, or lamb. This area is protected from sunlight and wind and is the last place to dry on the animal after it is born. The saying began in America and was well-known by the early 20th century.

A Cat Has Nine Lives

MEANING: cats seem very lucky and tend to survive things severe enough to kill them

IN CONTEXT: My cat fell off the roof for the fourth time this month. He really does *have nine lives*.

A cat has nine lives is an expression that began in ancient Egypt. Cats were revered in the Egyptian culture, probably because of their dexterity, agility, and ability to land on their feet from great heights. Cats were considered sacred animals with divine powers and were worshipped as gods. It was believed that Atum-Ra, the Egyptian sun god, gave life to eight other gods and embodied nine lives in one. On visits to the underworld, Atum-Ra took the form of a cat, which is most likely where the nine lives myth started. The number nine, sometimes called "the trinity of trinities," was also considered mystical and could have been associated with the revered cats. Bringing the expression to the Western world,

Shakespeare referred to the nine lives of a cat in his 1595 play *Romeo and Juliet*.

Beat around the Bush

MEANING: to deal with something indirectly and avoid coming to the point

IN CONTEXT: Just tell me what you really want and stop *beating around the bush*.

Beat around the bush is a phrase that began with hunting in medieval times. Wealthy noblemen engaged in hunting for pleasure, but did not want to put themselves at risk. They would employ men to assist them. The men's job was to flush out animals from within the brush so that the noblemen could shoot them. Often the men were sent into the undergrowth to scare out the animals, but in cases when they knew that dangerous animals were hiding, such as wild boar, they would beat around the bush, hitting it with a stick and making a lot of noise. By doing this, they hoped to scare the animals out into the open without actually endangering themselves.

Red Herring

MEANING: a misleading clue

IN CONTEXT: The police were following a *red herring*, but they're on the right track now.

Dating from the 18th century, **red herring** is an expression whose origins relate to the fish of that name. At that time herrings were caught in great numbers and, because there was no refrigeration, they were preserved by smoking. The smoking process turned the fish a reddish-brown color and also gave it a pungent odor. In an attempt to sabotage a fox hunt, people who were against the sport would drag the strong-smelling red herring across the trail to mislead the hunting dogs and throw them off the scent. The dogs would often follow the scent of the herring instead of the fox.

I'll Be a Monkey's Uncle

MEANING: an expression of shock, disbelief, or skepticism at an idea

IN CONTEXT: If the President stays in power at the next election, then *I'll be a monkey's uncle.*

I'll be a monkey's uncle relates to the theory of evolution postulated by Charles Darwin. As a follow-up book to his groundbreaking work *The Origin of Species*, Darwin published *The Descent of Man* in 1871. In it he suggested that man was descended from and closely related to apes. Creationism was widespread at the time, and his theory was greeted with almost universal derision and skepticism. In fact, his claims were considered so outrageous that people began saying, "well, I'll be a monkey's uncle" as a sarcastic response to ridicule his theory. It then started being used to show grave doubts about any improbable situation.

Birds and the Bees

MEANING: a coy euphemism used in reference to teaching a young child about sex

IN CONTEXT: My boy is about to turn ten, so it's about time I taught him about the *birds and the bees*.

The **birds and the bees** is an expression that has been used to describe nature in general for centuries. By the 19th century, prudish and reserved educators began using the habits of these animals as analogies to explain sex through the observation of nature—bees carry and deposit pollen into flowers, which is an example of male fertilization, and birds lay eggs, a visible example of female ovulation. The idea of adopting these natural metaphors for sex education may have been inspired by the lines of Samuel Taylor Coleridge's 1825 poem "Work Without Hope": "All nature seems at work...The bees are stirring—birds are on the wing...And I, the while, the sole unbusy thing, not honey make, nor pair, nor build, nor sing." Cementing the idea, the American naturalist, John Burroughs, wrote a set of essays in 1875 entitled *Birds and Bees, Sharp Eyes, and other Papers*, which presented nature to children in an easily digestible way.

Nest Egg

MEANING: savings that are set aside for later use, which a person tries to add to

IN CONTEXT: He lost his entire *nest egg* when the stock market crashed.

Nest egg is a phrase that has been used from as early as the 14th century in England. In those days before commercial factory chicken farming, chickens would lay their eggs in nests in the coop. As a

means of giving the chickens hope and encouraging them to lay more eggs, farmers used to place a porcelain or china egg in the nest or the coop area. This dummy egg was known as a nest egg and did often induce the chickens to be more productive. The expression was used to refer to someone's financial savings by the late 1600s.

Barking up the Wrong Tree

MEANING: pursuing the wrong course of action; making a mistaken assumption

IN CONTEXT: She had been trying to solve the math problem for an hour, but with the formula she was using she had been *barking up the wrong tree*.

Barking up the wrong tree is an expression that derives from hunting in America. In the early 19th century, men would go raccoon hunting. Because the raccoon is a nocturnal animal, dogs would be used to track them. In a panic to escape, the raccoons would often run up trees to the safety of branches out of reach of the dogs. Having picked up the scent of the raccoon, the dog would stand barking at the base of the tree to alert the hunter. But the raccoon is a cunning quarry and would occasionally trick the dog into thinking it was up a certain tree when it had actually escaped. It wasn't until the hunter had climbed the branches that he realized his dog was barking up the wrong tree.

Booby Prize

MEANING: a mock prize given to make fun of the worst player in a contest or game

IN CONTEXT: Jan has come last yet again so we should give her a *booby prize*.

Booby prize derives from the blue-footed booby, a South American bird that is known to be unintelligent and easy to catch. Sailors during the 17th century who first came across the birds found that they didn't try to escape when approached, and could be caught on deck with a simple noose and food as bait (this is the origin of the expression booby trap). Because of this, slow-witted sailors soon became known as boobies, and the prize given to anyone who came last in a contest was called a booby prize.

Final Straw

MEANING: a small and insignificant event that makes an entire situation intolerable

IN CONTEXT: I had hated my job for years, but when my boss berated me for taking a day off sick, it was the *final straw* and I quit.

The **final straw** is a contraction of the Arabic proverb, "it is the last straw that breaks the camel's back." It refers to a situation where a camel is so overloaded that by adding one last piece of straw its back finally breaks. "The last feather that breaks the horse's back" was a similar expression used

in England in the 17th century, but the final straw was popularized by Charles Dickens when he used it in his 1848 book *Dombey and Son*.

Bee's Knees

MEANING: excellent; the highest quality

IN CONTEXT: Have you tried that new Chinese restaurant in town? It's the *bee's knees*.

Bee's knees relates to the way in which bees carry pollen to their hives. Once the bee has extracted pollen from a flower, it carefully places it into sacs on the rear of its legs. Many believe the expression derives from the concentrated and rich pollen that is found around the bee's knees. Whether that is true or not, the phrase was first used in America in the 1920s when it became fashionable to use meaningless animal-inspired expressions to mean "excellence." There were many of them: the cat's pajamas, the snake's hips, the monkey's eyebrows, the eel's ankles, and the bee's knees.

CHAPTER 14
Tie the Knot: Till Death Do Us Part

Saved by the Bell

MEANING: a last minute rescue

IN CONTEXT: It was my turn to clean the house, but I got called away at the last minute to meet a friend so I was *saved by the bell*.

Saved by the bell has a number of conflicting explanations. One relates to boxing and the bell rung at the end of a round before a knocked-down boxer has been counted out to ten. If this happens, the boxer is allowed to continue fighting at the start of the next round. Another theory is that it stems from a guard at Windsor Castle in the 19th century falling asleep while on duty. He denied the charge and, in his defense, said that he had heard Big Ben chime thirteen times at midnight. The mechanism in the clock was checked and a cog had in fact slipped and he was correct—he had been saved by the bell. But the likely origin predates both of these and is the same as the explanation for dead ringer (page 233). In the Middle Ages, before the medical profession fully understood comas, people who displayed no signs of life were presumed dead and would be buried. Sometimes it was later discovered that they had been buried alive. People started attaching a string to their loved one's wrist that led to a bell above ground. If the person woke up underground, they were able to ring the bell and be saved. A number of designs for so-called "safety coffins" with bells incorporated were in fact registered as patents during the 19th century, lending weight to this theory.

Kick the Bucket

MEANING: to die

IN CONTEXT: Someone put poison in the dam and all the fish *kicked the bucket*.

Kick the bucket is sometimes said to originate from the theory that when people hang themselves, they stand on a bucket with a noose around their neck and then kick the bucket away. However, a more cogent explanation comes from the slaughtering of animals. In the 18th century, the wooden beam that was used to hang animals up by their feet for slaughter was called a "bucket." As the animals were killed they would often struggle and spasm, their feet kicking the bucket.

Tie the Knot

MEANING: to get married

IN CONTEXT: They'd been a couple for ten years so they finally decided to *tie the knot*.

While the expression **tie the knot** is symbolic of lasting unity, the use of knots during wedding ceremonies has existed for centuries in many cultures. During the times of the Roman Empire, the bride wore a girdle that was tied with knots. This was untied by the groom prior to consummating the marriage. This custom grew to actually tying the couple's hands together as part of the ceremony. Known as handfasting, the Celtics had a similar ritual whereby the hands of the bride and groom were tied together for a duration of one year plus one day in order for the marriage to be legal; the couple promised to stay together for this length of time as part of their marriage contract. A couple could not be married without tying the knot.

Dead Ringer

MEANING: a person or thing that closely resembles another; an exact duplicate

IN CONTEXT: Luke is a *dead ringer* for his father.

The origins of the expression **dead ringer** are often disputed, some citing horse racing, but it actually has a perverse beginning. Comas in medieval Britain were not fully understood by the medical profession, and anyone not showing signs of life was presumed to be dead. On some occasions when bodies were later exhumed, evidence was found suggesting the person had been buried alive—their fingernails were worn down and there were scratches on the roof of the coffin. To combat this frightening thought, people started putting a rod into the ground with a bell at the top and a string around their loved one's wrist. This way, if the person "came back to life," they could ring the bell and attract attention to themselves. This did actually occur from time to time, and if the person was later seen in public and anyone suggested a likeness to the person they used to know, it would be said that they are a dead ringer. By the late 19th century, the phase had come to mean anything that is an exact duplicate.

Head over Heels

MEANING: to be completely in love

IN CONTEXT: Within a week of meeting they had fallen *head over heels* in love.

Most often used in relation to being in love, **head over heels** actually began as "heels over head" in the 14th century. This made more logical sense, as it meant to be upside down, or to be so excited that you turn your heels over your head in a cartwheel or somersault. The phrase itself became inverted toward the end of the 18th century when Herbert Lawrence used it mistakenly in his 1771 novel *The Contemplative Man*: "He gave him such a violent involuntary kick in the face, as drove him head over heels." But it was the incorrect usage by Davy Crockett in 1834 that cemented the expression we use today and gave it romantic connotations: "I soon found myself head over heels in love with this girl."

Sleep Tight

MEANING: sleep well

IN CONTEXT: I was exhausted after a hard day's work, so I knew I was going to *sleep tight*.

Sleep tight originates from a time in England before spring mattresses were invented. In the early mass-produced beds, the straw mattresses were held together by ropes that were stretched across the bed frame in a crisscross pattern. After a while, the ropes would sag and it was necessary to tighten them. This was done with a forked iron or wooden tool, which was turned to wind the ropes tight. A mattress that had just been tightened was far more comfortable and allowed people to sleep tight. It was also stronger and less likely to break, which led people to advise newlyweds to ensure their beds were extra tight.

Lead up the Garden Path

MEANING: to deceive someone

IN CONTEXT: We were *led up the garden path* about the cost of the car hire. When they added all the extras on, the price was twice what the company advertised.

Also said as "down the garden path," **lead up the garden path** finds its origins in the early 1900s in England. Country estates at the time usually had acres of gardens that contained trees, hedges, and paths that would wind throughout. It was in the romantic parts of these gardens that gentlemen would traditionally propose to their sweetheart. Women knew this, so to be invited on a walk by a suitor was a positive sign and one that they were often keen to accept. However, it wasn't uncommon for some men to lead a woman up the garden path not to propose marriage, but merely to seduce.

CHAPTER 15
In a Nutshell:
Miscellaneous Matters

Gone 'round the Bend

MEANING: gone crazy

IN CONTEXT: The flies at the lake have been so bad that we've all *gone 'round the bend*.

Gone 'round the bend relates to the placement of mental hospitals. In Victorian England in the 19th century, a number of hospitals were built to house the mentally disabled. Long, straight driveways were characteristic of stately homes so that they could  be viewed with envy from the front. Conversely, so that they remained unseen from the road, mental asylums were built at the end of long curved driveways. If someone was committed to an asylum, they had literally gone around the bend.

Pidgin English

MEANING: a simplified language used to communicate between two people who do not have a common language

IN CONTEXT: I was buying a wooden carving in Africa and managed to get the deal done by speaking *pidgin English* with the locals.

Pidgin English originated in the late 17th century. It was developed by British traders in China as a way of doing business without having a language in common. The expression actually means "business English," and came about because of the mispronunciation of the English word "business" by the Chinese. They pronounced it "bijin," and this led to pidgin. The language they used was a combination of both English and Cantonese and was spoken as a second language. Over the years, the phrase pidgin English developed to mean any two languages that are pieced together to aid effective communication.

Down in the Dumps

MEANING: depressed or unhappy

IN CONTEXT: Going back to work after such a good holiday made me feel *down in the dumps*.

Down in the dumps is an expression that has been used since the 16th century. The earliest reference is in Thomas More's *A Dialogue of Comfort against Tribulation* in 1553. It then became widespread after its usage in *The Taming of the Shrew* in 1596 when Shakespeare wrote, "Why, how now, daughter Katharina in your dumps?" Where the expression actually originated is unclear, but the dumps was a common medieval term meaning "dejection" or "depression." It was probably taken from Europe, where various languages have similar words—the German *dumpf* means "gloomy," the Swedish *dumpin* means "melancholy," and the Dutch *dompig* means "damp" or "hazy."

On Skid Row

MEANING: a squalid area inhabited by vagrants and derelicts

IN CONTEXT: John started drinking so regularly that we thought he was headed for *skid row*.

On **skid row** is an expression that originated in the American lumber industry of the 19th century. Large tree trunks were hauled by rolling them along tracks made of greased logs that were laid crosswise. This was known as the "skid road," because the trunks skidded across the logs. The timber industry was booming at the time, and many men came to the logging towns to find work. The large numbers of single men created a demand for bars and brothels, which would spring up in a certain part of the town. This area also became known as skid road due to the imagery of someone slipping, or skidding, down in society when falling victim to these vices. By the 1930s, skid road had been altered to skid row, and the wider use was born.

In a Nutshell

MEANING: concisely; in a few words

IN CONTEXT: Chris was always long-winded so I told him to give me the facts *in a nutshell*.

In a nutshell is said to originate from an ancient story described in AD 77 by the Roman scholar Pliny the Elder. The story goes that the philosopher Cicero witnessed a copy of Homer's epic poem *The Iliad* written onto a piece of parchment and enclosed into the shell of a walnut. While this is thought to be impossible, it is believed that important documents were folded and inserted into walnut shells and bound so that they were waterproof and could be taken long distances without damaging them. Shakespeare refers to the expression in his 1603 play *Hamlet*, which immortalized the phrase.

Play Hooky

MEANING: to be absent from school or some obligation without permission

IN CONTEXT: It was a sunny day so Jeb decided to *play hooky* from work and go the beach.

Sometimes spelled "hookey," **play hooky** arose during the mid-19th century when school attendance became compulsory in America. There are a number of possible explanations for the phrase. It may be a contraction of the older expression hook it, meaning "to escape or make off," or it could be related to the slang word hook, meaning "to steal," as in stealing a day off school. A third possibility is an association with going fishing. Missing a day from school was like "getting off the hook," the way a fish does when it escapes, and a common pastime for children when they played hooky was to go fishing.

Wait for the Other Shoe to Drop

MEANING: to await a seemingly inevitable event

IN CONTEXT: Oscar knew his wife had saved enough money to leave him, so he was *waiting for the other shoe to drop*.

Wait for the other shoe to drop began with the American manufacturing boom in the late 19th century. In large cities like New York, apartment housing became common. These dwellings were all built with similar designs, with bedrooms typically located above one another. It was common to be awoken late at night by a neighbor removing their shoes in the apartment above. The person below would often wake when the first shoe dropped on the floor and made a loud bang. Already disturbed, the person would then wait for the inevitable noise of the other shoe hitting the floor.

The Third Degree

MEANING: intensive questioning or interrogation

IN CONTEXT: When I met my wife's parents, they really gave me *the third degree*.

The third degree comes from the Freemasons, a centuries-old fraternal organization in Britain. In Masonic lodges, there are three degrees of membership. The first is known as Entered Apprentice, the second is Fellow Craft, and the third is Master Mason. As the third degree is far more challenging than the first two degrees, the candidate is subjected to rigorous questioning and examinations before he receives the third degree of Master Mason. By the 19th century, the third degree had come to mean any kind of interrogation.

Chop and Change

MEANING: to keep changing what you do or plan to do, often for no apparent or logical reason

IN CONTEXT: After months of *chopping and changing*, the company decided to go back to the original accounting system.

The expression to **chop and change** sprung up during the 15th century, and since it originated, the meaning has been used in the same sense that we use it today. Chop is an archaic Old English word meaning "to exchange" or "change suddenly." To chop and change meant to change suddenly and then change again. The first written example is from the 1485 *Digby Mysteries*—"I choppe and chaunge with symonye, and take large yiftes (gifts)."

Blown to Smithereens

MEANING: to explode or destroy something into tiny pieces

IN CONTEXT: There were only three boats that attacked the fleet and they were *blown to smithereens* within ten minutes.

Always used in the plural, **blown to smithereens** is of Irish origin. Smithereens derives from the Gaelic word *smidirín*, meaning "small or tiny fragments." The expression was in common usage by the early 19th century and was first written in Francis Plowden's 1803 book *An Historical Review of the State of Ireland*, where he wrote, "If you don't be off directly…we will break your carriage in smithereens, and hough your cattle and burn your house."

Round Robin

MEANING: something that operates in a rotational manner, such as a circular petition or letter; a sporting tournament where each player plays all others

IN CONTEXT: The organizers decided to change the tennis tournament to a *round robin* instead of sudden death.

Round robin stems from 17th-century France, when peasant revolts were rife. Whenever the King received a petition for change, which contained a list of signatures, he would generally call in the top few people on the list, who were thought to be the ringleaders, and behead them. Still desperate to petition the King but not wanting to be killed, the peasants devised a concept they called a rond ruban (meaning "round ribbon"). It was a length of ribbon joined to form a circle, which the petitioners would sign. This disguised who had signed first and protected everyone. This practice was also adopted by sailors in the 18th century. Mutiny was a serious offence but a captain was unable to hang his entire crew, so any complaints were made by signing a circular petition. The term adapted to round robin and was first recorded in *The Weekly Journal* in 1730: "A Round Robin is a name given by seamen to an instrument on which they sign their names round a circle, to prevent the ringleader being discovered by it."

Dressed to Kill

MEANING: dressed in expensive or stylish clothes

IN CONTEXT: When Bob came to pick up Sue for the dance, he was *dressed to kill*.

Dressed to kill has its origins in a letter from the English poet John Keats to his two brothers, George and Thomas, in 1818. In it he wrote, "One chap was dressed to kill for the King in Bombastes, and he stood at the edge of the scene in the very sweat of anxiety to show himself." The expression received wider acclaim from an 1881 interview for the American newspaper the *Cambridge Tribune*, when an army recruit was asked how he felt about his brand new uniform. "I am dressed to kill," was the soldier's simple reply.

Riding Shotgun

MEANING: to travel in a car's front passenger seat

IN CONTEXT: It was going to be a long journey so I was glad to be *riding shotgun*, as it was far more comfortable there than in the back seat.

Riding shotgun derives from the days of stagecoach travel. In America during the 19th century, postal express messengers became known as "shotgun messengers" because they rode up the front of the stagecoach next to the driver and carried a loaded shotgun. A shotgun is a useful weapon in close quarters in an ambush situation, as it scatters multiple lead pellets and makes it likely to at least skim the target. Stagecoaches were often confronted by armed bandits or dangerous animals such as bears, and the person riding shotgun was there for protection. The expression was in common usage by the early 20th century, but became widespread with the rise of Wild West films in the 1950s.

In a Jiffy

MEANING: a short period of time

IN CONTEXT: Don't go anywhere Joe, I'll be back *in a jiffy*.

While some people presume that the jiffy in the expression **in a jiffy** is a slang term, it is actually a scientific unit of time. The first technical usage of the term was by the American physical chemist, Gilbert Newton Lewis (1875–1946). He defined a jiffy as the time it takes light to travel one centimeter in a vacuum, which is approximately 33 picoseconds—a very small unit of time. Since then, a jiffy has been redefined as different measurements depending on the field of study, but in all instances it is a very small period.

Mumbo Jumbo

MEANING: nonsense; meaningless or complicated speech or writing

IN CONTEXT: There was so much legal *mumbo jumbo* in the contract that I couldn't really understand it.

The expression **mumbo jumbo** began with the early explorers of Africa in the 18th century. Francis Moore was one of the first Englishman to travel into the interior of the continent and in 1738 wrote the book *Travels into the Inland Parts of Africa*. In his book he describes how the men of one tribe, the Mundingoes, employed a legendary spirit to ensure obedience in their women. "The women are kept in the greatest subjection," he wrote, "and the men, to render their power as complete as possible, influence their wives to give them an unlimited obedience, by all the force of fear and terror. For this purpose the Mundingoes have a kind of image eight or nine feet high, made of the bark of trees, dressed in a long coat, and crowned with a wisp of straw. This is called a Mumbo Jumbo; and whenever the men have any dispute with the women, this is sent for to determine the contest, which is almost always done in favor of the men." It was this passage that brought the term mumbo jumbo to the masses and by the mid-1800s, the phrase had come to mean any meaningless rantings.

Warm the Cockles of Your Heart

MEANING: a feeling of affection, satisfaction or pleasure

IN CONTEXT: Looking at her baby boy for the first time *warmed the cockles of her heart.*

Some suggest that **warm the cockles of your heart** stems from the Latin *cochleae cordis*, meaning "ventricles of the heart," cochleae being similar to the word "cockle." But the likely origin dates back centuries. The heart was long considered the thinking and emotional center of the body, because of the flutters that are sometimes experienced. The ancient Greek philosopher, Aristotle, was the first to hold this view. When a person was excited and their heart pumped faster, the rapid movement of the blood created a warming effect, so warming the heart came to mean what it does today. Then during the 17th century, anatomists likened the shape of the ventricles of the heart to the cockle, a marine mollusk, and the full expression was born.

Butter Someone Up

MEANING: to ingratiate yourself to someone with flattery

IN CONTEXT: I didn't really like the coach, but I had to *butter him up* because I was desperate to play on Saturday.

Butter someone up is an expression that dates back to ancient India. The Hindus always wanted to keep their gods happy so that the gods would  watch over and protect them. Ghee was a clarified butter that has been used in Indian cooking for centuries, and is still in use today. The Hindus had a custom of throwing balls of ghee at the statues of their gods to butter them up. They did this to keep the gods happy generally, and also if they were seeking a particular favor.

Without Batting an Eyelid

MEANING: to take a situation in your stride, without displaying any emotional response

IN CONTEXT: Margaret *didn't even bat an eyelid* when I told her I was moving out.

Always used in the negative, **without batting an eyelid** is another expression that derives from the linguistic world. The word "bat" comes from bate, an obsolete English word, which in turn comes from the Old French *batre*, meaning "to beat the wings" or "flutter." When a person reacted to something of note without showing any surprise or emotion, to the extent that they didn't even blink, or flutter, an eyelid, it was said that they didn't bat an eyelid.

An Ax to Grind

MEANING: a selfish or ulterior aim

IN CONTEXT: Harry claimed to be disinterested in the outcome, but I knew he had *an ax to grind*.

The expression **an ax to grind** is credited to Benjamin Franklin, one of the Founding Fathers of America. In his autobiography, Franklin wrote an anecdote about a man who wanted his ax ground. A blacksmith agreed to do it, but only if the man turned the grindstone himself. The man did this, but soon feigned fatigue and gave up, making the duped blacksmith finish the job for him. Franklin's story didn't mention the phrase, but in 1810 Charles Miner, an American congressman, published an essay entitled "Who'll Turn Grindstone?" It detailed a similar story that was clearly based on Franklin's account and included the expression an ax to grind.

Read between the Lines

MEANING: to discern a meaning that isn't explicitly stated or obvious

IN CONTEXT: Finn's girlfriend canceled their date three times, so he *read between the lines* and realized it was probably over.

Read between the lines is an expression that derives from the early days of cryptography in the 19th century. Cryptography involves encoding messages into seemingly innocuous text. One of the first techniques used to pass codes was to write the intended message on every second line and have an unrelated innocent message across all the lines. When read normally and in its entirety, the story was simple, made sense, and did not reveal any code, but when just the alternate lines were read, the code was deciphered.

To Egg On

MEANING: to encourage or urge someone, usually to do something foolish

IN CONTEXT: My brother always *eggs me on* to drive faster.

The phrase **to egg on** has linguistic origins. Originally "to edge on," it derives from the Old Norse word *eggja*, meaning "to edge" or "to incite." To eggjan, or edge, someone was to encourage them. The expression had adapted to egg on by the 1500s and was being used in its current sense by that time.

Cloud Nine

MEANING: a state of extreme happiness and contentment

IN CONTEXT: Ever since Josh bought his new house he's been on *cloud nine*. I've never seen him so happy.

 Generally preceded by "on," **cloud nine** is an expression that began in the 1930s. Between that time and the 1950s, the US Weather Bureau divided clouds into nine classes. The highest class, cloud nine, was the cumulonimbus cloud. Those clouds tend to be white and fluffy in appearance and reach up to 40,000 feet. Because of their height and attractive nature, to be on cloud nine came to symbolize floating in a carefree manner. The expression became widespread because of the popular US radio adventure series *Johnny Dollar*. It ran from 1949 to 1962, and whenever the hero in the story was knocked unconscious, he was transported to cloud nine, where he was revived.

Spitting Image

MEANING: an exact likeness

IN CONTEXT: Gloria is the *spitting image* of her mother.

While some believe "spit" is a corruption of "spirit" in this expression, **spitting image** is actually a contraction of "spit and image." The saying began with the idea of someone being formed from the spit of another, so great is the similarity between them. It was as though one had been spat out of the other's mouth—the "spit and image." The first known written reference to this was in George Farquhar's 1689 play *Love and a Bottle*, which included the line "Poor child! He's as like his own dadda as if he were spit out of his mouth." Spit and image had evolved to spitting image by the early 20th century.

On the Grapevine

MEANING: via informal means of communication, particularly gossip

IN CONTEXT: I heard *on the grapevine* that Patricia and Ernest are about to break up.

On the grapevine owes its origins to the early days of American telegraphy. Samuel Morse invented the telegraph, which was first used in 1844. The invention was widely recognized as a useful means of rapid communication, and many companies across America rushed to put up telegraph lines. In their haste, some cut corners and used trees instead of fixed telegraph poles to save money. However, the movement of the trees stretched the wire, often leaving it tangled. A notable instance of this was in California, where people likened the tangled wire to the local grapevines. The expression "on the grapevine" developed its current meaning during the American Civil War, when messages transmitted via the telegraph were sometimes unreliable.

Warts and All

MEANING: the entire thing, not concealing any unsavory detail

IN CONTEXT: I knew the news wasn't going to be good, but I told him to give it to me *warts and all.*

Warts and all derives from Oliver Cromwell, the Lord Protector of England in the 1650s. Cromwell instructed the royalist painter, Sir Peter Lely, to paint his portrait. As was usual at the time, Lely's style was to flatter his subject, showing them in the best possible light with all blemishes removed. Cromwell was known for being opposed to personal vanity and he issued the following instruction to Lely: "I desire you would use all your skill to paint my picture truly like I am and not flatter me at all. Remark all these roughness, pimples, warts, and everything as you see me, otherwise I will never pay you a farthing for it." Lely did just that, and the portrait includes a mole above Cromwell's eye and a large wart below his lip.

From the Wrong Side of the Tracks

MEANING: the less desirable part of town

IN CONTEXT: The gang *from the wrong side of the tracks* was accused of the robbery.

From the wrong side of the tracks is an American expression which dates from the 19th century. Towns and cities at the time grew up along the newly built railroads. The tracks would usually divide the towns. The more affluent residents would live upwind from the railway station, avoiding the fumes and loud noises from the trains, while the poor townsfolk would live in houses downwind. It was downwind of the station that factories were also generally built, adding to the grime of area. Upper-class people came to refer to the poor who lived in the other part of town as being from the wrong side of the tracks.

On the Wagon

MEANING: abstaining from drinking alcohol

IN CONTEXT: Don't offer Kate any wine, she's *on the wagon*.

It has been suggested by many that **on the wagon** derives from when prisoners, who had had their last drink, were transported from the Old Bailey in London to the gallows on a wagon. Some even suggest that the criminals were sometimes given "one for the road," a final drink before they were hanged. It is now widely accepted that these explanations are fanciful. The expression is actually a contraction of "on the water wagon." In the early 20th century, water wagons were used in America to dampen dusty streets. At the time, the consumption of alcohol was high, and people who had vowed to give it up would crowd around waiting for the water wagon to arrive to quench their thirst. Some would even ride around town on the wagon drinking the water in an effort to stay away from alcohol.

Whole Kit and Kaboodle

MEANING: the whole thing; everything

IN CONTEXT: My new car has all the latest technology—satellite navigation, digital radio, auto-sensors—the *whole kit and kaboodle*.

Sometimes spelled as "caboodle," the **whole kit and kaboodle** has been in existence since the late 19th century. It began as "kit and boodle," the two words having similar meanings. The kit in the expression meant "a collection of tools or possessions that might be carried in a kit-bag." Boodle comes from the Dutch word *boedel*, meaning "a group or collection, usually of people." The phrase developed to the whole kit and kaboodle, which meant "everything in your possession." The earliest citations of the current saying are all American, and date from 1884, when it was used in the New York newspaper, *Syracuse Sunday Standard*.

Close, but No Cigar

MEANING: to fall just short of success

IN CONTEXT: They needed three points to win the basketball game, but the ball bounced off the frame and missed. It was *close, but no cigar*.

Close, but no cigar is an expression with American origins. Fairgrounds and circuses were popular during the 19th century. Like today, they always had sideshows with competitions that involved hitting a hammer against a pad to make a bell ring, shooting in galleries, and throwing down moving pins. The main prize offered for winning these competitions was usually a large Havana cigar, which was much sought after at the time. Contestants who just missed out on winning heard "close, but no cigar." The saying was used colloquially in America by the 1930s.

Have a Hunch

MEANING: have an intuitive or instinctive feeling

IN CONTEXT: They didn't seem happy together and I *had a hunch* they would soon break up.

Have a hunch takes its origins from gambling in early 20th-century America. There is a centuries-old superstition that hunchbacks are possessed by the devil, who gave them the power to foretell the future. Gamblers, who are notoriously superstitious, believed that rubbing the hump on a hunchback before placing a bet or playing a hand of cards would bring them good fortune. It is unknown whether this superstition was ever put to the test and, if so, whether it was successful, but as a result, to have a hunch came to mean what it does today.

To Be Blackballed

MEANING: to be voted against; someone who is not acceptable or is outcast

IN CONTEXT: Jack applied to be a member of the club but he *was blackballed* because of his bad reputation.

To be blackballed derives from the London gentlemen's clubs of the 18th century. New applications for membership were assessed by a ruling committee and then put to the members for a secret vote. Every existing member of the club had to vote, and the votes were cast by placing either a white or black ball into a container. White balls meant acceptance and black balls meant rejection. One single black ball was enough for the application to fail, and nobody ever knew which members were in opposition.

Artwork Credits

All interior artwork are from www.shutterstock.com.
Individual photographers are as follows:

page 4 © mssa

page 7 © mad_snail

page 9 © dvarg

page 12 © lanteria

page 15 © netkoff

page 17 © retroclipart

page 21 © blambca

page 23 © natalia

page 26 © balazik

page 33 © rtro

page 34 © pixeljoy

page 37 © Olena Gai

page 38 © bsd

page 41 © onot

page 43 © onot

page 44 © oorka

page 46 © nekrasova anastasiya

page 48 © uncle leo

page 51 © mjosedesign

page 53 © retroclipart

page 54 © alex74

page 56 © dima groschev

page 59 © Alexander P

page 61 © dn br

page 62 © retroclipart

page 65 © jennifer johnson

page 67 © MSSA

page 68 © patrimonio designs ltd

page 71 © kovalevska

page 73 © infini

page 74 © aleks melnik

page 77 © hein nouwens

page 79 © gor malovic

page 81 © lineartestpilot

page 84 © morphart creation

page 86 © dedMazay

page 88 © olga rotko

page 90 © aliaksei zykau

page 93 © morevector

page 94 © ss1001

page 97 © phant

page 98 © vadimmmus

page 100 © alex kuzyuberdin

page 102 © advent

page 106 © ron and joe

page 108 © mhatzapa

page 113 © ira cvetnaya

page 114 © arak rattanawijittakorn

page 116 © untitled

page 119 © visual generation

page 120 © aleks melnik

page 122 © john t takai

page 124 © visual generation

page 126 © goldstock

page 128 © ananas

page 131 © christos georghiou

page 133 © nikiteev konstantin

page 135 © chuhail

page 137 © artstada

page 138 © knut hebstreit

page 141 © michele paccione

page 144 © itvega

Index of Sayings

About the Author

Andrew Thompson divides his time between Australia and England. A lawyer by trade, his obsession with finding out the truth about aspects of the world that we take for granted has led him to accumulate a vast body of knowledge, which he has distilled into book form. The author of the two Ulysses Press bestsellers *What Did We Use Before Toilet Paper?* and *Can Holding in a Fart Kill You?*, see all of Andrew's books at www.andrewthompsonwriter.co.uk or at Twitter @ AndrewTWriter.